D1491574

It's your law

a series of books dealing with various aspects
of the law prepared and edited by
the Law Society

SERIES EDITOR   *Graham Lee*

The company director
and the law

OTHER TITLES IN THE IT'S YOUR LAW SERIES

The company director and the law

John A Franks

Oyez Publishing Limited

THE AUTHOR
John Franks, a senior partner in an old-established firm of London
solicitors, has had extensive experience in practice both in England
and Europe. He is also a Fellow of the Chartered Institute of
Arbitrators. He has written *The Companies Act 1967—An Introduction*
and many articles on a wide variety of legal topics.

ISBN 85120 507 0

First edition   1973
Second edition   1977
Third edition   1981

Published by Oyez Publishing Limited,
Norwich House, 11/13 Norwich Street
London EC4A 1AB

Filmset by Vantage Photosetting Co. Ltd.
Southampton and London
Printed and bound in Great Britain by
Biddles Ltd, Guildford and King's Lynn

Contents

Preface

to first edition

The title 'company director' evokes many images. It conjures up the figure of the Victorian railway promoter with his top hat, mutton-chop whiskers and cigar, the seedy operator of dubious money-making schemes and the dynamic world-trotting top executive. It is the accolade of the self-employed window-cleaner and the struggling middle grade personnel of some industrial corporation. To join the board is to arrive, to achieve status; to become chairman and managing director of his own company, be it ever so humble, is to establish a man in his own eyes as a success.

The point is that, like birth, the appointment has consequences. There are duties and obligations as well as rights.

It is a strange fact that, though there is a complex concept fairly fully developed of the commercial business company, much of the terminology in current use is inexact or ambiguous. It relates to economic eras which have long passed, if they ever existed. The workers in a factory look to the governor of the business as the owner of it, whereas in truth the chief executive, who personifies that character in their eyes, is in law only an employee like themselves. The shareholders are often presented as a group of hard-headed or rapacious individuals driving the company on to extract the maximum in dividends and capital profits. The board of directors is regarded as a mixture in varying proportions of these self-seeking individuals; even worse it often includes money men—accountants and merchant bankers—who have adding machines where their hearts should be and abacus beads in their brains. Then there are the silver haired fuddy-duddies who drive up, querulous, to meetings in Rolls-Royces and sink into amiable mumblings over directors' port.

So much for the images of the 'media'. In practice the director must be alert. The plain reality is that by the device of the company the control of a business is divorced from the ownership in law. The powers and responsibilities are vested in delegates who in big corporations come to regard the management of the company as an end in itself. The director is thus the supreme manager and the manager supreme. From this it follows that the economic and other interests of the organization and its various grades of employee tend to become more important than those of its owners. The director may of course still be an owner of an interest in the company or be associated with a major interest in it, but he does not need to do so. It must also be emphasized that this book is intended for directors, and covers their duties and obligations as such. There are many interesting questions from the point of view of shareholders, particularly minority shareholders, but that is another story.

The permutations are endless, from the director who is the principal shareholder and only employee to the member of the board of the public company quoted on the Stock Exchange who does not have a single share but only a service contract. But the duties of all directorships in law are standard and should be appreciated. Far too often the assumption is made that with the limited liability company there can be no further responsibility on the part of the individual. It is not so. Not only are there commercial pressures on directors to pledge their personal credit if they wish the company to be accepted by other business concerns, but failure to observe the ground rules can cause the directors to incur personal liability. There are many other important matters of which directors should be aware, apart from the need to ensure proper running of the company in the interest of its enterprise, and, being aware, take advice on the implications. The purpose of the book is to set out guidelines for directors, not to make them instantly into lawyers, accountants, company secretaries or merchant bankers. No statutes, no cases, no footnotes interlard the text. Practitioners' manuals can be very, very hard to use as an introduction to a subject—productive more of sleep than knowledge! As you pore over the tortuous phrases you may get it wrong. If you are sitting comfortably then read on—it is hoped that you will find it interesting.

Introduction

to third edition

This book is written for company directors as a class and those who
wish to join them. The intention is to provide a guide through the
ever-thickening minefield of rules and codes. As such, it indicates the
safe paths of conduct and where potentially explosive situations may
lie. If for good business reasons it is desired to take short cuts or
venture on excursions, this book can do no more than utter warnings
and suggest that expert professional guidance shall be sought to defuse
situations before the director or his company get singed, if nothing
worse. The view has been taken that by making an issue of the
qualification of a secretary employed by a public company ultimate
responsibility has been shifted on to him to a greater extent. The
Companies Act 1980 has not only amended the existing Companies
Acts, but has ventured on to new areas for statutory regulation. In part
this is in the name of harmonization within the European Community,
in part it is due to the desire to make directors more responsible legally
as well as morally. In this latter endeavour it tends, like much that is
produced by Parliament, to add to the burdens of honest men.

Much of this is due to rejection of the belief of the traditional
English Common Law that the buyer ought to be careful before he
parts with money. For those who simply want to earn their livelihood
with the least possible complication, the old English approach had its
merits.

In preparing this edition the fact that, like all modern statutes of any
importance, the 1980 Act will come into operation in parts at different
dates has been ignored. It is assumed that the Department of Trade

will have it all working soon enough. In an attempt to simplify, the position before, during and after changeover has only been indicated and not explained in detail; this is for other, more weighty tomes. The fact that explanations may be too brief or the statements liable to exception or qualification is inevitably a problem where a vast subject is summarized in so few words. For while the reader may nod a little through some passage or other, even more soporific books can be had, for those who wish or have to master the subject of company law.

For those who need to know about the offences which are committed if breaches of duty occur, there is a table at the end of the book. It has been comprehensively revised, listing these in an alphabetical order with the limits of punishments that can be imposed.

JOHN A FRANKS

Chapter 1

What is a company director?

The history of public limited companies began in the nineteenth century, but the private limited company was only introduced in 1908 and was really part of a pattern at the turn of the century to confer on the smaller business enterprises the advantage of limited liability. At the same time the limited partnership was introduced, with its split between active partners who were liable to creditors generally and limited partners whose sole connection was to provide working capital, and who were not liable for more than the amount they agreed to provide. As might have been expected, the businessman preferred the private limited company because it meant the active partner could instead be a director and escape from personal liability to creditors. To this day, in a commercial discussion, participators in companies frequently refer to each other as partners and really consider their business enterprises as types of partnerships. This is commonly the case where companies have been bought 'off the shelf' from formation promoters. When the business enterprise proves to be successful, the parties find it extremely difficult to understand the differences which arise from a company structure. Far too often the discovery of what are their rights and interests comes as a shock and a personal disaster, because of the gulf between what the parties thought was their position in relation to each other, and the facts in law, which were never explained to them.

A working director is an employee of the company who can be sacked from employment like any other employee. Apart from the technical provisions governing removal from his appointment as a director, he has no better position and in many cases a worse position than other employees, because of the way the terms of service are defined and the additional responsibilities that this status confers.

A director as such has no interest in the assets of the company and in turn no personal liability for the capital or trading debts of the company. It is possible by contracts or guarantees to make him liable; it is even possible with a limited liability company to provide that a particular director shall be liable, but in the ordinary way there should be no such liability unless the director has been guilty of misconduct usually involving fraudulent or criminal activities.

It is also within the powers taken by the Inland Revenue, the Customs and Excise and the National Insurance Commissioners to claim from directors personally monies that have not been paid by the company in certain circumstances, particularly monies which were or should have been deducted from employees' wages.

It is possible to incorporate companies without limited liability—the only form allowed in practice for certain professional activities—but even so the director is not personally liable as such, but only if he is a shareholder, and even in that his liability for debts is no different from that of any other shareholder.

Liability for the debts of the company is the responsibility of its owners, who are referred to as the members of the company and who are commonly the shareholders. If the company is incorporated without limited liability, goes into liquidation, and cannot pay its debts, the members may be called upon to do so by the liquidator. In eighteenth- and early nineteenth-century books, references may be found to prosperous men being ruined by the collapse of companies in which they were shareholders. This made the owning of shares in a business enterprise extremely hazardous. Limited liability was introduced, among other things, so that money could be raised by selling shares in a company to the public, on the basis that the purchaser had only to provide a fixed sum of money for his share or shares. A share could be fully-paid-up at the outset and so be called a fully-paid-up share, or part of the money could be left outstanding as a reserve to be called in case of need. This second is called a partly-paid share. This is the basic concept which applies to all limited companies and which has been developed in Europe in the same way. But within the European Economic Community a new approach is developing towards groups of companies, particularly where operations in one state are controlled by a subsidiary owned by a holding company in another. Here the law may look beyond the veil of incorporation of the subsidiary, at the holding company itself, on the grounds that subsidiaries have no free will and engage in concerted action that is deliberate in operation. This approach has arisen out of the question of European rules against price-fixing but may be extended into other spheres. On the other hand it has been held that the documents of a foreign subsidiary with a local board are not under the control of the holding company in England.

Memorandum and articles

Each limited liability company has to have a constitution, and a great deal of thought and ingenuity went into the arrangements for making the organization of companies comparatively cheap and simple. The old idea of a private Act of Parliament was replaced effectively in 1856 with an Act under which the company was created as a separate legal person by registration, with a certificate of incorporation acting as the birth certificate.

The Act of 1856, which was followed by the Act of 1862 and other Acts, laid down that the constitution should be divided into two parts:

(a) The Memorandum of Association, and (b) the Articles of Association.

Both of these have to be signed up by the potential first members who are called the subscribers. They operate in law as a deed of agreement between the company and all future shareholders. Certain particulars of the first directors and shareholders have to be provided at once. Such a body has to have an address at which notices can be given to it and its registered office has also to be notified.

There are important differences between a public limited company and a private company, although it now has to have only two subscribing shareholders, in the same way as a private company. A public limited company (plc) has to have a qualified secretary who is the official responsible for seeing rules are observed. Above all else, a public company is not allowed to carry on business or exercise any borrowing powers without a certificate that it has the requisite minimum issued share capital under the Companies Act 1980 which has replaced the old prospectus requirements. Nevertheless in offering shares to the public (after incorporation and certification) a public limited company will still require a prospectus—or statement in lieu—which is a very complex document that requires highly skilled advice on its preparation and compliance with the requirements of the Stock Exchange if a quotation is desired. It contains a number of commitments and representations about future business by the board of directors. A private company is not allowed to offer shares to the public and by definition under the 1980 Act a private company now is any company that is not a public company.

As a result of the Companies Act 1980 all existing public companies that wished to retain status by becoming a public limited company (a plc) have to re-register with formalities which include making a formal application for change of name during the transitional period. Directors of companies so affected need professional advice as to the steps to be taken on the facts of their particular company during that period as, apart from anything else, there has to be a shareholders' resolution passed by a three fourths majority if the company is to re-register as a private company unless the capital is below the authorized minimum of £50,000.

The modern statutes dealing with incorporation today, the Companies Acts 1948 to 1980, follow these basic principles. A company in its Memorandum has to set out the following: (i) the name of the company. If it is to be a public limited company the name must end with these words or 'plc'. If it is to be a private limited liability company the name must end with the word 'limited' or 'ltd' unless it has special licence to omit the word 'limited'; (ii) whether or not the members are to have limited liability; (iii) that its registered office is to be in England or Wales, or in Scotland; (iv) what are the objects; (v) what is the share capital.

(i) The name of the company is settled on incorporation and can be changed by resolution but it must first always be approved by the Department of Trade. The certificate with the name is commonly displayed in a frame at the registered office, although this is not necessary. In the case of companies with registered offices in Wales which choose to use Welsh equivalents the terms would be 'cyfyngedig' and 'cyf' for limited and 'cwmni cyfyngedig cyhoeddus' and 'ccc' for public limited company. What the company must do is to have its name legibly displayed outside every place of business. The name must also be engraved on the seal and has to appear on all business correspondence, advertisements and circulars. This includes all financial documents such as cheques and bills of exchange, promissory notes, invoices and receipts. If the name of the company does not appear on all such documents it is an offence, and a person who signs such a document is liable himself if the company fails to pay. Furthermore a director or manager who signs when the name of the company is not given correctly or only in an abbreviated form can be made liable himself. Some companies, usually formed for charitable or philanthropic purposes, apply for and obtain consent to omit the word 'limited' from their name.

(ii) Limited liability must be claimed by inclusion in the Memorandum, otherwise the members of the company are liable on insolvency.

(iii) The registered office cannot be moved out of Scotland or out of England and Wales, but can be moved between England and Wales.

The original choice has to be made on incorporation and the exact address notified to the Companies Registry. Any subsequent change should be notified within fourteen days. Wales is included in England for statutory purposes, but a company which has a registered office in Cardiff now states in the Memorandum that the registered office will be in Wales or in Cardiff. Similarly a company can declare that it is registered in England or in London.

(*iv*) The objects of the company are supposed to represent the purposes which the company is incorporated to fulfil. Unfortunately, owing to what is called the *ultra vires* doctrine which was developed in the nineteenth century, a company was not allowed to carry on any business or do any act which was not expressly permitted by its objects clauses. It became the practice, which still persists, to adopt a 'kitchen sink' wording, to include every kind of business and every kind of act which might remotely be required in the course of the trade. There is a custom, although it has no strict legal basis, to describe the real business in the first two or three sub-paragraphs of the objects clause. There are model clauses in the Companies Acts, but these are in a simple form which ignore this problem. Since 1948 it has been possible to alter the objects of a company, subject to certain technicalities, and it has been argued from this that the *ultra vires* doctrine is no longer of importance, but particular care has still to be taken to ensure that the company does not fall foul of it. Two particular common traps are the need for the express power to pay pensions to directors, who are not regarded in the same category as employees, and the need for the power to give guarantees between parent and subsidiary companies. The position is also modified by the rules of the European Economic Community, by which a contract between a company and another person who enters into the contract in good faith is valid and binding on the company, even though it is beyond the powers conferred on the company by the Memorandum. The rule is that the other person is entitled, without investigation, to assume that the company has the necessary power. Furthermore, the fact that he ought to have known of the limitation of the powers of the company, or of a director or other person to act on behalf of the company, still does not invalidate the contract. It is for the company to prove that the other person really knew the legal position, or that he did not act in good faith. This throws a grave personal burden on the directors and the secretary. If the company does something which is beyond its powers, or the directors commit it to something which they were not supposed to do, the remedy of the shareholders, who cannot now rely upon the transaction being nullified, is to sue the directors and secretary for misfeasance. In such cases, unless the shareholder can prove bad faith, the court may still relieve the director or secretary from liability. There is a special discretion where it is shown that an officer acted honestly to give relief even in the case of negligence. As the secretary now has to be a person with requisite knowledge and experience, whilst some or even all of the directors may escape responsibility on the basis that they relied upon the secretary, the secretary can have no such excuse.

(*v*) The share capital of a company represents the ultimate fund for paying liabilities to creditors. Accordingly there are strict regulations to define and identify the capital committed to the company by its members, either by way of payment or guarantee. A company has to have a nominal amount which it may issue, or in the case of a company limited by guarantee a nominal number of members who each guarantee a sum of money. Public companies must have the authorised minimum share capital. No companies limited by guarantee with a share capital may be constituted since the 1980 Act and in consequence no new company limited by guarantee can become a public company. The capital is stated in the Memorandum in the terms of the amount and the number of shares into which it is divided. The shares may be divided into separate classes, such as ordinary and preference shares, and the separate rights of each class may be set out in this clause. It is, however, usual to give these particulars in the Articles of Association.

It is common for companies to require the whole of the amount of the nominal value of a share to be paid up on issue or by instalments within the year. But directors may for one reason or another decide not to call for all the money. In such cases the shares remain partly paid and the uncalled balance represents a reserve or resource which can be required if the company needs it or becomes insolvent. Public companies have to require payment of at least one quarter of the nominal value plus the whole of any premium except for bonus shares or employees' share schemes. These are schemes for genuine employees or former employees of the company or group and their spouses, widows, widowers or children (including step-children) under the age of eighteen.

In the case of public limited companies the first subscribers to the Memorandum have to pay cash for such shares (including any premium) and there has to be a minimum paid-up share capital of £50,000 (which can be varied by a statutory instrument). If not paid in cash, this must be for consideration which is properly valued by competent valuers. A mere undertaking to do work or perform services cannot be accepted in lieu of cash. Furthermore the capital has to be preserved and if the assets fall below one half, the directors must give twenty-eight days notice for a shareholders' meeting within fifty-six days of any director knowing this fact. This means that the matter will be public knowledge because the notice will go to the Stock Exchange. It is a draconian provision because the effect will be to cause a loss of credibility with suppliers, financiers and customers even though the company may be solvent. The directors must therefore watch this aspect very closely indeed. The responsibility of monitoring such matters is that of the company secretary, who has to keep all records and accounts subject to the direction of the board, who can charge one or more executive directors as finance or managing director with obligations in this area. Again, because share capital of all limited companies must be preserved as a fund, share capital can only be returned to members under a scheme approved by the court. Legal advice should be taken on any such proposal. It also follows that such a company cannot buy and sell its own issued shares except perhaps as part of a scheme approved by court, although a board can forfeit or accept surrender of shares for non-payment of share capital by someone to whom shares have been issued, and this can include employees' shares until paid for completely. Redeemable preference shares which are a special type of capital can be repaid under the rules in accordance with which they are issued. It is possible, though not likely, that a company may acquire shares in itself without valuable consideration in which case those can be sold and the proceeds would increase the balance of surplus assets available for distribution to the shareholders, subject to the terms of the gift.

In the past when the Memorandum could not be altered, it was the practice to include fundamental share rights in the Memorandum. This practice still continues since it is more difficult to change rights set out in the Memorandum. It is also sometimes the practice to include in the Memorandum some special declaration, for example in the case of an investment company that it should not engage in trading or any dealing business, or in the case of companies—often unlimited—which are allowed to carry on some types of professional practices, that the company should observe the disciplines of the profession concerned.

The Articles of Association are really the byelaws of the company, as distinct from the constitution set out in the Memorandum. In the Articles are all the rules which govern the way the business of the company is to be conducted internally. A model form is set out in Table A Part I of the Companies Act 1948, which is automatically applied to every company incorporated under that and the subsequent Acts except in so far as it is excluded or varied. Every company which did not want to be a public company had to adopt Part II in addition, or rules similar to it. However, as the law now stands, every company which is not a public limited company is a private company prohibited from offering shares or debentures (including loan stock) to the public or allotting them for such sale. To be a private company it is no longer necessary to impose restrictions on the right to transfer shares or limit the number of shareholders. Part II of Table A has been repealed but still applies to any company which had been registered with articles that adopted it until such time as the company amends its articles, as do the old provisions of Part I even though these have been amended by the 1980 Act.

Companies formed under the earlier Companies Act have applied to

them the Table A which was set out in that Act. It is therefore
necessary to be very careful when examining the Articles of any
company to make sure what exactly is applicable; the Articles have to
be read as a whole. If the Articles conflict with the Memorandum,
then that overrules the Articles. A further problem is that under the
various Acts there are prohibitions or compulsory variations of the
Articles which will override anything to the contrary in the
Memorandum or the Articles. This is particularly a problem with the
older private companies which commonly have not brought out an
up-to-date edition of their articles showing these involuntary changes.
On important questions expert legal advice is necessary.

In the Articles—supplemented in the case of most private
companies by Table A—are the rules for altering share capital,
conducting meetings, the types of resolutions possible, directors,
their meetings and affairs, accounting, dividends and debentures, as
well as provisions on how to alter the Articles. It is possible for a
company to have no Articles of its own at all and simply adopt Table A.

The Articles form a contract between each member and the
company which is binding on them as such, but the Articles are not a
contract between members, so it is the company that is the person to
enforce it. The Articles confer no rights on outsiders, although they
may be evidence of the intention of the company to make an
agreement. As the Articles are a public document, anyone dealing
with the company is deemed to know and understand them. He is
protected so long as what the company or its directors and officers are
doing is not inconsistent with the Articles.

A company is not liable for the act of an individual who is a director
or secretary, unless it has presented him as possessing the authority.
In the case of a managing director, the Articles will expressly set out
his power to sign contracts. In the case of contracts signed on behalf of
the company by someone other than the managing director it is good
practice to ask for a copy of the Board resolution approving the
contract. Such a copy resolution should be certified by the chairman
and the company secretary. On the other hand, a company secretary
can be expected to deal with minor administrative details such as

ordering hire cars, and the company will be liable for this action even though the secretary was not expressly authorized to order them.

The shareholders

The shareholder is a member of a company having a share capital, with his interest in the company governed by the Memorandum and the Articles. He becomes a member in one of five ways:

(a) by subscribing originally;
(b) by application for shares followed by allotment;
(c) by transfer;
(d) in the case of the personal representatives of a dead member, by registration of an assent; or
(e) in the case of a minority shareholder, who with others represents no more than 10 per cent of the shareholders of the same class, by order of the court on a reconstruction or by the operation of the compulsory take-over provisions of the 1948 Act.

In every case except the last, the membership involves agreement. In the last case it arises out of the agreement for membership of the original company. What is sometimes overlooked is that the modern form of transfer, developed for government stock and public companies quoted on the Stock Exchange, is often used for private companies. As far as the company is concerned this does not involve any act of agreement by transferee. In most cases this may not matter, but it is now possible, using this form, to make someone a shareholder in a company without his knowledge or consent. This is most important in the case of private companies which control the admission of members and may even impose special restrictions on them—such as non-competition—or whose shares may not be fully paid. Directors, who have to approve the changes on the register, should be satisfied that the transferee has agreed to accept and be bound by the Articles.

Membership of a company is determined by the share register, which is one of the official records which the company has to maintain and from which particulars have to be provided to the Companies Registry and to the members in annual returns and reports. However, each shareholder is entitled to a properly completed share certificate. This is his proof as against the company that he is entitled to these shares. It is possible in theory for a company to issue bearer shares, that is to say shares to which the exclusive title is the certificate and not the register. For many years the issue of new bearer shares was prohibited or severely restricted in this country for reasons connected with the control of the economy. Share transfers have to be stamped, except in special circumstances, with a stamp duty based on a small percentage of value, whilst bearer shares are only subject to the payment of a special composition fee on issue. The special circumstances in which it is possible to obtain exemption from stamp duty have to be certified to the Inland Revenue, and relate to such cases as a transfer from a nominee to a principal or from a trustee to a beneficiary.

Members of a company have their rights and interests conferred on them by the Memorandum and Articles. Normally the entire conduct of the business is passed over to the directors. The rights of the members are then only to have the affairs of the company properly administered, to receive information in accordance with the Acts, to approve the accounts, reports and dividends, elect directors, appoint auditors, and determine remuneration—although in practice this is usually left to the Board. Members also have to authorize allotments of shares or rights to shares (unless specific authorities are given to the directors which can only be valid for up to five years at a time). The general principle is that ordinary or equity shareholders are now entitled to first refusal on any new issue of ordinary shares. The rights can be limited by the Memorandum or Articles of a public company (although it is required procedure for companies under Stock Exchange listing agreements) but are excluded altogether for private companies. Directors also have to obtain approval from members in general meeting of any acquisitions or disposal by a director of substantial property or non-cash assets in a deal with the company or any subsidiary. Any transaction which involves more than £1000 has to be approved unless it is insignificant when compared with the net assets of the company or the group, that is to say less than 10 per cent of the net assets. However, if the transaction involves more than £50,000 the director always needs approval. Another right of members is to decide whether payments may be made to employees or former employees on the cessation or transfer of the whole or any part of the business undertaking of the company or any subsidiary, unless that power is given to the directors by the constitution contained in the Memorandum or Articles of Association. The decision will be by simple majority at members' meeting unless provision is made for some other form of resolution in the constitution.

The board of directors

It is the job of the board of directors to carry on and supervise the business of the company. A company does not have a body or a brain of its own and can only operate through agents. This presents problems for the law. As a judge once pointed out when discussing crime by a company: 'You cannot hang its seal.' So although by a fiction a company is a legal person, it is the directors who embody it. As long as the directors do nothing illegal nor breach codes of conduct to be observed by directors they cannot themselves be made liable for anything they do on behalf of the company, unless it is done in their own name or in an incorrect rendering of the company name. If a director makes a contract without disclosing that it is for the benefit of the company, or does so in the wrong name, the company can still approve the contract, take the benefit and indemnify the director. The other party, once he knows of the situation and if he wants to sue on the contract, usually has a choice. He can either sue the person who signed it or the company, but not both.

In their handling of the business and assets of the company, directors must always satisfy themselves that what they are doing is reasonably part of carrying on the business. They must act in good faith, and they should be satisfied that what is being done is for the benefit of the company and will promote its prosperity. This must be watched particularly carefully when a company is part of a group, but has either shareholders apart from the holding company or separate sources of finance. Indeed, directors could find themselves in personal trouble if a subsidiary company became insolvent and a major trade supplier, whose only claim was against the company, could show a breach of this duty. This might well arise as part of a re-grouping exercise, if for example a freehold was passed over at book value to a group property company, and later there was an insolvency. Each director also has a duty of overall supervision and is not supposed to ignore wrongdoing in another department.

There are many sinister tales of directors who make secret profits for themselves. There have been many court cases fought over this. In law, which is often logical, directors are supposed to conduct the business of the company for the benefit of the company, that is to say the collective body of shareholders. Directors are therefore expected in this sense to behave as trustees for the company in respect of its money and its property. If directors make away with or misuse the funds, it is a breach of this trust. This does not stop a director buying up shares that are on offer even if he has special knowledge, but he must not use his powers as a director to benefit at the expense of the other shareholders. Directors of public limited companies (in common with all other individuals who have access to unpublished information which could affect the price of a share on a stock exchange) are subject to a code of conduct which carries criminal sanctions controlling dealings with shares on a recognized stock exchange. This also applies to dealing in quoted shares with an off-market dealer who makes a market outside the stock exchange. There are no special penalties in relation to the shares of private companies nor in respect of private deals in the shares of public limited companies so long as they are not done through a market, although the Stock Exchange has a model under which a director should not deal in the two months preceding the preliminary announcements of half yearly and annual results as well as any time when a director has unpublished price sensitive information.

It is the board of directors who give instructions in the name of the company. As long as there is a formal resolution authorizing this, a director can speak and act in the name of the company and appear anywhere on its behalf. But a company must instruct a solicitor to represent it in the High Court, and the solicitor, who has no right to argue a case before a judge in the High Court, has to instruct a barrister to speak for the company. Statements on behalf of a company are usually made by the chairman or managing director, although notices of meetings are sent out by the secretary.

Business names and registration

In all business correspondence a company is supposed to give its correct name, but like any individual it can carry on business under a business name. So for example a tea shop trading as 'The Ever Hot Tea Pot' may be carried on by the Shaftesbury Tea and Coffee Company Ltd. The same rule applies to everyone not carrying on business in his own name, so that such a company should register the trade name together with its own name, in the Business Names Registry. There is also the further rule that in the case of all companies incorporated after 1929, when the rule was introduced, not only must the business letterheads show the name of the company, but also the names of all its directors. It is only necessary to disclose foreign nationality against a director's name on the letterheading if he is a national of a country not in the European Economic Community.

As a result of the legislation for entry into the European Economic Community, companies have to show, in addition to their name and registered office, the registration number of the company, and the place of registration. This last is to be welcomed because there are several separate company law jurisdictions for registration in the United Kingdom, and it will be most convenient to know the correct register for making searches. The registries in common use are those

in London, Edinburgh and Belfast, but companies incorporated
abroad for use in activities in the United Kingdom, whilst avoiding
United Kingdom taxes, are not uncommon. Furthermore, if a limited
company is one that has been allowed to dispense with the word
'limited' as part of its name, a statement that it is incorporated with
limited liability must also appear. In addition, if any mention is made
by the company of share capital, such as 'incorporated with a nominal
capital of £1,000,000', then the paid-up share capital must be
mentioned, '£100 paid up' for example.

A new power has been taken to stop overseas companies carrying on
business in their corporate name if the Minister thinks it undesirable.
Notice by the Minister had to be given within six months of 18 April
1977 or the date either when the company first delivers documents for
registration on establishing a place of business in Great Britain or
seeks registration in a new name. If a different name has to be used,
then for all purposes that is deemed to be the corporate name. A
company has two months in which to comply with a notice (unless
withdrawn), failing which trade must cease. A foreign corporation
which carries on business in Great Britain under a business name
which does not consist of its corporate name alone has to register
under the Registration of Business Names Act, and the Registrar has a
discretion to refuse any name he considers undesirable. Any person
responsible for management is to be treated and made liable for
compliance as if he was an officer of the company. If such a company
ceases to trade it can apply for removal. These powers are intended to
prevent, for example, companies incorporated abroad with the word
'Bank' in their name, being allowed to use that name if the
Department of Trade consider that they should not claim to trade as a
bank apart from the controls exercised by the Bank of England under
the legislation controlling banks and companies that take deposits.

The formation of a company

Forming a company with the Memorandum and Articles, setting up
the first board of directors and getting it going is a complicated

procedure. This involves the working out of relationships between the shareholders and the directors, and laying down the rules under which the share capital is to be organized, both immediately and for the future. The first shareholders are supposed to reach agreement on all these matters and then sign—subscribe is the official term—the Memorandum and Articles of Association for the company, and agree to take up shares. This signed copy has to be lodged at Companies House with a fee to the State for registration; so have various other forms setting out the capital, the names and addresses of the first directors and secretary, who have to sign as accepting, the registered office, particulars of the allotment or division of shares and what has been paid or given for them. A declaration of due compliance with the statutes must be made by the solicitor engaged in the formation, or by an officer of the company. After a few days for processing the documents, the Registrar will issue the certificate of incorporation. This is the birth certificate. If it is a private company, business can then commence. Changes of directors and secretary must be notified within fourteen days. Notice must also be given of changes in particulars. This means every time a director, in respect of whom a list of other directorships has been given, accepts a new directorship or resigns one shown on the list, a change notice must be given. The Registrar is under a duty to acknowledge receipt of these notices. A company is at all times to have a registered office, and notice of the intended situation must also accompany the application for incorporation, and notice of change given.

A company has to have copies of its Memorandum and Articles available for reference, and these are usually printed after incorporation from proof copies used for the purpose of incorporation. It also has to keep certain records by statute, which are called the statutory books, and a seal with which to complete documents. If it is a public limited company, business cannot start and borrowing powers shall not be exercised until the registrar issues a certificate of satisfaction as to the initial capitalization or re-registers it as a private company. It has been common practice to form all companies as private companies and change over to public companies afterwards and this may continue as a practice under the new 1980 procedures for public limited companies. The switch is by special resolution to change the Memorandum and Articles of Association to those of a public limited company, and then by filing documents at Companies House. This consists in practice of a portfolio comprising the special resolution, the Memorandum and Articles as amended, a statement by the auditors of net asset value, the balance sheet with an unqualified auditors' report, a valuation report (where the consideration for the issue of shares was not cash), together with a statutory declaration by a director, or the secretary, of due passing of the special resolution and of no change between the balance sheet date and the date of application reducing the net assets below the aggregate of the called up share capital and undistributable reserves. This latter requirement could prove difficult unless the balance sheet date was close to the application date or the business realising substantial profits.

There are matching provisions to change public limited companies over to private companies as well as transitional provisions for public companies to become public limited companies or private companies. Minorities who have at least 50 members or represent 5 per cent of the share capital or any class or (in case of a company not limited by shares) of the membership, have special rights which enable them to object to court within 28 days of the resolution.

A company with a registered office in Wales can have its documents of incorporation in Welsh and can end its name with the word 'Cyfyngedig'. In that event its business papers must state in addition in English that it is a limited company and a certified English copy of its Memorandum and Articles must be filed. All documents can be filed in Welsh but must be accompanied by similar translations. An alternative is to have the document in English accompanied by certified Welsh translations.

It is most important that on the formation of a company the parties should be fully advised as to the results of the arrangements then being made, which can have far-reaching effects in the future. The relationships should be worked out and the documents drawn up accordingly. Very often people starting up in business prefer to save money and spend as little as possible on the formal organization of their affairs. The minimum State fee plus the stationers' charges for the statutory books and seal which the company has to have, and the printers' charges for the Memorandum and Articles makes this a substantial sum in any event. It has therefore become common to purchase new companies from the stock of a formation agency. There are a number of such agencies. They keep a variety of companies for different types of business activity which are available for a composite fee complete with final printed copies, books and seal. The Articles are usually in a standard form which the agency considers should suit most people, and the individuals who use these services can be in business as a company instantly.

The troubles come later, either when the business is successful and the parties find that their rights are not what they thought they were, or when it is unsuccessful and one party finds that he has much more to lose than the other. Sometimes these matters are sorted out by sensible discussion, and the disappointments or losses are accepted philosophically, but sometimes the cases come to court. Almost invariably when the parties go to their solicitor or accountant they are told that matters are not as the directors had thought. To be fair to the agencies, their job is to sell a cheap commercial product, not to advise. If an agency does advise, and its advice is not sound, it may be that the agency could be sued, but this is, however, most unlikely. In some ways these instant companies are as much a source of mischief as the home-made will on a stationer's form. Professional advice should be taken from a solicitor at the outset, or as soon as possible after the company has been set up, rather than wait until the troubles build up and become obvious. Again, as with home-made wills, it is very often the widow who suffers.

The promotion of a company

A company promoter is not an officer of the company as such. He is a concept that belongs more to the Victorian past, when a company would be promoted by the holder of some concession or contract, to build a railway or to exploit some mineral deposit in Britain or abroad. Far too frequently the forecasts would be over-optimistic or the prospects over-sold. A statutory code was created to restrict the offering of shares to the public to authorized dealers, in other words stock brokers who are controlled by their own professional organization and code, and to dealers licensed by the Department of Trade. This move together with the strict rules as to liability for fraud and other charges if statements in prospectuses are not true, plus the procedures for complete investigation required as a condition for dealing in shares on the Stock Exchanges, has eliminated the flamboyant characters of the past. Promotions of public companies are now undertaken in the main by brokers, merchant banks and issuing houses. Usually companies have to prove an established profit record before quotation is permitted. It has always been a rule that a contract signed on behalf of a company prior to incorporation was wholly without effect in law. The contract if so signed had to be ratified by both parties after incorporation. Under the new European Communities law where a contract is made on behalf of a company not yet incorporated, except as otherwise agreed, the person signing the contract will be personally liable.

For private companies, the concept of the promoter is in the main inapplicable, since shares are not offered to the public at large, and companies are usually organized or re-organized by people who have mutual interests. Nevertheless, a person seeking finance through introductions—advertisement for sale of shares is not allowed—may be liable for the truth and accuracy of any statements he may make in order to encourage investment. With private companies, except where the parties are already known to each other and familiar with the business to be undertaken, investors will normally require their own solicitors and accountants to investigate and check the position of the company. It is an offence for a private company to offer its shares or debentures to the public or allot or agree to allot shares with the view to them being so offered. There are, however, exceptions where the offer is regarded as a domestic concern because the offer is to existing holders or to some class of them or employees under an employees' share scheme or the families of holders or employees. Curiously, 'family' for this purpose not only includes spouses, widows and widowers but children of any age (including step-children) and their descendants and family trustees. It does not include parents or siblings. If a number of people are likely to be involved in receiving a duplicated letter or circular legal advice should be taken. It may be desirable to have the circular first approved by the Department of Trade even though it is thought to be exempt as a domestic concern in case in practice the circulation goes wider than originally intended.

Chapter 2

A director and the shareholders

As mentioned already, the director is responsible for the running of the company. This means more than just a responsibility to the shareholders. His duties are not merely to them, but also to all people dealing with this artificial creature of the law that we call a company. If a director does something which he is not authorized to do, such as borrowing for the company more than the Articles allow without the consent of shareholders, the director may be personally liable to the lender. This liability arises because he would be assumed to have held himself out as having the power to do the business, that is to say 'warranted his authority'.

Directors have to be properly identified. Not only their names but their nationality, if it is not British or of one of the countries within the European Economic Community, must be stated in the business correspondence and documents, as well as notices filed at Companies House when they take or give up office. The definition of a director has been extended, and now means not only the directors appointed as such but includes anyone on whose instructions the directors are accustomed to act. Under the Articles the directors usually have the full authority to run the company. If a controlling or large shareholder, who is not a director, gives instruction to directors outside formal resolutions in general meeting, that shareholder ought to be shown as a director.

Indeed a person on whose instructions the directors are accustomed to act is now called a shadow director and bound by the same rules of conduct where conflicts of interest, loans from the company and dealings with it are concerned. A shadow director must give notice to the directors of any interest he has in any business to the same extent as a director and any service agreement has to be open for inspection. Consultancy agreements with former directors would have to be considered in this context. Boards should take legal advice on any marginal case of this kind. By law, public companies must have at least two directors, and a private company one. The maximum and minimum numbers which the particular company may have are set out in the Articles. Usually the minimum number is kept up as a board of directors cannot properly act without it, except to appoint another director. Business done by an outsider, who is unaware that a company does not have the right number of directors, may still be valid.

Directors must also check whether the Articles of Association require a share qualification. Originally it was thought that, since directors represented shareholders, they themselves should have a minimum investment in the share capital. It was common to provide that a director should have his shareholding on appointment, or buy it soon after. There is now a statutory period of two months after which he is disqualified until he gets his holding. Furthermore a director who sells his shares qualification automatically vacates office upon registration of the share transfer. The fashion has now turned away from this idea of a compulsory share qualification, because it meant that capable men who did not have the initial capital to acquire a minimum shareholding could not be recruited to the board. A director on appointment should always check this point, although if he sells his qualification shares by mistake he can apply to the court for relief against the consequence. Strangely, fashion, or perhaps taxation, has now come in a full circle, because many companies introduced share incentive schemes to enable executives, including executive directors, to acquire an interest in the share capital of the company. Whether or not directors should follow the capital fortune of the company, the new rules about insider-dealing make it difficult for a director to realize any part of a holding he may have or invest money in the company without first taking professional advice as to what is proper in particular circumstances.

Usually directors have all the powers of the company, except to do things which either under the statutes or under the Articles of Association can only be done by the company in general meeting. Anything that the company can do, the directors can do. If allowed by the Articles, directors can delegate their powers to a committee drawn from the board, and one director on his own can constitute a committee. Minutes have to be kept for the committee which is subject to the same procedure rules as the board. The directors must remember that in using powers they are in the position of trustees and what they do must be for the benefit of the company alone. If the directors act in good faith, a court will not intervene at the request of a shareholder to alter the decision of the directors.

Such is the power of directors, under the normal form of Articles, to carry on the business of the company, that shareholders cannot pass a resolution to reverse or change a decision of the directors made in good faith, unless the shareholders alter the Articles of Association. The only resolutions directly about the conduct of the business that the shareholders can in practice pass are decisions as to whether or not to sue in the name of the company, approve the allotment of shares or sanction the employment of a director for a period exceeding five years.

Directors must be properly appointed but once a person is said to be a director by the company through stating this in a letter or on its letterheading, or giving notice to the Companies Registry of his appointment, then the company is liable for his acts as a director. The question of whether a person is or is not properly a director is a decision of the majority of the shareholders.

The power of an individual director to contract for the company is limited, particularly in relation to himself, and except as expressly allowed in the Articles he cannot enter into contract for his own benefit. This rule is to prevent any conflict of interest, except that which the shareholders have allowed for in the Articles. This does not prevent a director from taking up shares in the company. Unless the Articles allow it, the shareholders may direct the company to bring an action to set aside the sale of any part of the assets of a company to a director or even the purchase of property from a director, if the fact that it was his property was concealed. This extends to transactions with other companies in which the director has shares.

The Articles of Association usually provide for directors to disclose any conflict of interest to the board, and abstain from the board's proceedings relating to it. In some companies the Articles do permit them to speak at these proceedings, and sometimes even to vote, provided prior disclosure has been made.

Much difficulty is caused by secret benefits. Directors are not supposed to make any profit other than the salary, bonuses or commissions which have been duly approved. Anything which is obtained as a secret benefit can be claimed from the director by the company. The rule is strict in the sense that if the director does something for a bribe which is not paid, the company can still sue for it. Any contract which the company has made can be set aside and any monies paid or rights or goods given, can be recovered. So long as the director makes proper disclosures, the Board or the shareholders can of course allow the contract.

Insider-dealings

The most difficult cases of what the Americans refer to as 'insider-dealing' occur when directors do not take direct advantage from some other party to a contract, but instead use their knowledge to buy or sell

shares in the company, or to deal on the Stock Exchange. Morally it
may be wrong to allow directors to take advantage of their special
knowledge to purchase shares from executors of dead shareholders, or
any other willing seller, without telling of good news that is to be
released, but in law there is no objection. It is for the seller to make his
own decision. If shareholders are approached to sell and given wrong
or misleading information, that is another matter. Criminal charges
and civil claims can follow if the shareholder afterwards finds out that
he has not been dealt with fairly. The problem comes on the Stock
Exchange when prices quoted go up and down according to the news
that has reached the dealers.

Directors can therefore allow rumours to go unheeded, and then
buy or sell in the market—perhaps through nominees—on the basis
of their own reliable information. As one American lawyer pointed
out, large profits can be made in such circumstances although
individual shareholders may lose only a small sum each on their
shares. It is little use any individual suing the directors, because the
amount he is likely to recover from them will not justify the expense.
In the United States, to meet this problem, the law has been developed
by the idea of the 'class action', on the basis of which one individual
can sue in the name of all the shareholders and the damages recovered
are so divisible. The key to the situation is that in American law the
courts do not award costs. The lawyers act on a speculative basis,
taking a percentage, perhaps 20–30 per cent of the damages, if any,
recovered. British company directors whose companies decide to seek
a quotation on an American Stock Exchange must be prepared to face
allegations and claims that are quite startling in this respect. It is said
that one director was sued for stating 'no comment' to the Press when
asked to confirm or deny that his company had a certain action in
mind, on which the board had taken a decision.

The problem with claims for 'insider-dealing' of this character is not
that they may be justified, but the extent to which such cases may be
brought without any real justification simply for the sake of a
compromise payment. The payment of 'nuisance value' money to get
rid of the claim, rather than have the trouble and anxiety of having to

deal with it, cannot only involve large sums of cash, but also, like the Danegeld, encourage new claims. In this country the directors' obligations to give particulars of share dealings and holdings were extended with the idea that publicity may in fact inhibit such conduct. However, the law has now been developed to prohibit and apply criminal sanctions to Stock Exchange or other market dealings by directors, officers or employees—or for that matter anyone who has access to private, sensitive information in shares of the company with which he is connected or in any other company which is involved with it.

So far as directors are concerned, it was accepted in the course of the discussions in 1980 that it was quite impossible for directors to avoid situations where they have conflicts of interest. A director may well find, therefore, that as a trustee of shares in the company he might wish to sell, but that by virtue of his access to information it would seem improper. This has been resolved on the basis that while it is an offence for a director to advise anyone upon dealing in the shares of his company, if the trustees or personal representatives of which he is one decide to buy or sell then concurrence by him is not an offence. Presumably unless one of the trustees is a competent adviser, advice will always be taken. In such cases or where he is a sole personal representative (who would have, therefore, only to deal on advice) a director should avoid expressing views except valid and genuine reasons which are not directly related to the prospects of the company. Similar duties are also imposed on individuals whether company secretaries and other officers, employees, professional advisers or even business colleagues.

The general duty of confidence is demanded from individuals as well as from directors (who have it by virtue of their office) who occupy positions which may reasonably be expected to give access to unpublished, price sensitive information and which it would be reasonable for them not to disclose except in the proper performance of their functions. Anyone in breach who is convicted may be ordered to pay compensation or make restitution in respect of any resulting gain, loss or damage. These rules all apply to individuals dealing in the market, but not to companies, for example merchant banks, although partnerships are vulnerable. The rules prohibit dealings within six months of an individual being connected with the company who knows unpublished, price sensitive information. It must also be reasonable to expect a person so connected and in the position in which he is connected not to disclose to anyone except for proper performance of his functions. The position of the office tea lady was cited as an extreme example. It was suggested that the difference lay in a subjective test, which is another way of suggesting that it is necessary to apply common sense! The point is that the person who gets the information (the tippee) also commits an offence if, being an individual, he deals on a recognized stock exchange during the six months from getting the tip. It follows that if a chairman, at the bar of his golf club, says that his shares will go through the roof in the next two months, a tippee present may be guilty of an offence if he buys shares for himself but not a limited company of which he is a director, although he might be guilty of incitement. Another strange position is that of a supplier to a company who may get confidential information beyond that which relates to his own transactions with the company. If he is an individual or a partnership and deals then in theory he commits an offence, but if he is in business as a limited company which buys and sells, the company does not. Fortunately there are exceptions which exempt individuals from liability against doing anything otherwise than with a view to making a profit or loss (for himself or any other person) by use of the information, transactions entered into in good faith as a receiver, liquidator or trustee in bankruptcy. There are special rules for Crown servants and others in such positions and also for international bond issues such as jobbers on the Stock Exchange; these rules do not prevent an individual involved in a transaction from completing it. This is of particular relevance in respect of take over bids. If an individual alone or with others contemplates making an offer he is not to deal in the shares of that company if he knows that the fact about whether or not the bid is made is price sensitive information. Neither is he to tip anyone else although he can discuss this with anyone who he believes will not use the information improperly. Of course this does not stop a bidder from building up a strategic holding with a view to making a bid, and buying and selling whilst doing so.

There are company lawyers who look forward to the right set of circumstances which will enable cases to be fought and won for civil remedies including damages for breach of these prohibitions quite apart from any prosecution. This may become of increasing importance particularly because, with the approval of the court, shareholders may sue, in the name of the company, wrongdoers who are or control the board of directors. If a majority of shareholders have a complaint, an action can in theory be brought on behalf of the company against the board or members of it. However, in the ordinary way the company as such suffers no damage for which it can sue if the share price fluctuates, or even if, in the absence of fraud, information in a board circular or statement is incorrect. American law is quite different because unlike those in the United Kingdom, limited companies in the United States can buy and sell their own shares.

In an effort to curb leaks of information and provide a framework of authorized procedure the Stock Exchange and the Take-over Panel require early disclosure of impending take-over bids. This is intended to be coupled with a temporary suspension for, say, twenty-four hours to enable the board to draft a statement. The most persistent problem area has been not actual leaks but inspired guesses about what is happening, leading to speculative movement. The problem is that for a short period after the board has made its decision and before the statement or heads of agreement can be finalized there is an ever-widening circle of persons with sensitive information. It follows that boards should announce when talks have reached a point where the offer is reasonably certain and negotiations are about to be extended beyond a small group, eg when family shareholders are asked to support the board decision to recommend acceptance. Further, as soon as the board reaches the stage when it appears that it will be approaching others outside the original negotiators, and before it can be sure of the support it wants, it should inform the Quotations Department so that a temporary suspension can be arranged while

these steps are in process. Bidders are frequently shy but are enjoined
not to press for secrecy until sure of obtaining control. The willingness
of the Quotations Department to provide for temporary suspension
will assist in this respect, because the board, under the cover of such a
temporary halt, can complete its soundings and finalize the
paperwork. Only then will full disclosure have to be made. This, of
course, creates new problems, because announcements may well be
made before contractually binding agreements are made. These can
encourage a different type of speculation, based on information or
suspected information as to the way the bidder or a competitor will
behave once dealings resume after announcement. Nevertheless the
procedures (coupled with the new rules for announcement of dealings
by directors and earlier disclosures on transactions with important
holdings) ought to reduce in practice the demand or need for
investigations on account of suspected improper insider-dealing.

The share register

The directors have to ensure that the company, in addition to making
returns to the Companies Registry, keeps proper records of the
ownership of shares, and dealings in them. There must be a register
showing the names and addresses of members and the dates when they
became members. It can be a loose-leaf ledger or a record capable of
being reproduced in legible form, for example by a computer. In the
case of the company having a share capital it must also state the
amount of shares or stocks held, with the distinguishing or reference
numbers of each share, if the shares are numbered, and the amount
paid or treated as paid on them. This record has to be kept at the
registered office or if kept somewhere else in England or Wales, or
Scotland if it is a Scottish company, notice has to be given to that effect
to the Companies Registry. In addition if a company has more than
fifty members, and particularly those private companies who issue
shares to employees can come into this category, it must also keep an
index with the register. The register has to be open to free inspection

by members and to the public on payment of an inspection fee. Copies must be provided of the register and index within ten days, but there is no right to make copies on inspection. The court will always order inspection although the right to inspect terminates on a winding-up. Companies can close their registers for not more than thirty days in a year, provided prior notice is given by advertisement.

The directors are responsible for seeing that the register and index are properly kept and are liable to penalties and default fines if these are not so kept. Usually the duty is delegated to the secretary or an officer specially appointed and termed a registrar, but in either case the directors are responsible to see that entries are made properly and duly authorized by them. A person on the register is held out as a shareholder, and is liable for calls for any balance due in respect of shares, unless he is entitled to ask the board to remove his name and does so promptly. Creditors as well as shareholders may call upon the courts to order the rectification of a share register. Usually the board are advised not to change an entry on the register once made, unless it is an obvious clerical error, except with the order of the court or unless the persons requesting the change provide an indemnity which is guaranteed by an insurance company or a bank. When shareholders change their address due notice should be taken of this, as well as changes of name by marriage or death, so long as the share certificate is produced.

The directors should not allow any trusts to be noted on the register. Their concern is only with the persons whose names appear as members whatever the capacity in which these persons own shares. This general principle is now subject to an exception in the case of companies whose shares are quoted on a recognized stock exchange. It is now a requirement of the standard conditions of the Listing Agreement, which regulates the quotation on the Stock Exchange as between the company and the Stock Exchange, that price sensitive information be passed on to the Share and Loan Department. The view seems to be that any acquisition of more than 5 per cent by a nominee holder is price sensitive, and the directors ought to exercise their powers to discover the identity of the principal and pass this information on by way of an announcement to the Stock Exchange. If members want to transfer shares they must complete a share transfer. The transfer has to be in the form set out in the Articles or authorized by the board. There is a modern form specially designed for trading in shares or government stock on the Stock Exchange. It does not have to be under seal and need only be signed by the seller or transferor.

As printed, this is not really appropriate for private companies, which should require the transferee to sign and acknowledge his willingness to be bound by the conditions of membership which, unlike with a public company, restrict dealing with the shares. Private companies do not now have to restrict rights of transfer. If a transferee is registered who has not agreed to be bound by the articles he could argue that he is not restricted to selling to someone else. In any event, this form is not suitable for shares that are only partly paid.

Share transfers do not now have to be under seal. When shares are transferred the certificate must be lodged with the company—unless it has been put on deposit in advance. Formal procedures for lodgement are worked out in some detail by registrars or secretaries for public companies, but directors need not be concerned with them except to find out what the procedure of their company may be. If the board approve the transfer in the case of a private company they will pass the transfer, cancel the certificate lodged, and issue a new certificate to the transferee, provided the transfer has been properly completed and stamped. It is an offence to pass an unstamped transfer. Stamp duty on share transfers is payable on a scale related to the amount paid for the transfer unless the transfer is exempt.

Usually it is the job of the secretary to check the transfer and confirm;

(a) that it conforms with the certificate lodged, and the certificate agrees with the record;
(b) what the stamp duty should be;
(c) the particulars of the transfer and any special information the board may require when considering the approval of the transfer;

(d) whether the transfer proposal is in accordance with the Articles;

(e) the particulars of the new certificate.

Once the transfer has been approved by the board (or the committee appointed to deal with transfers) it should be registered and the new certificate dated, signed, sealed and checked. Normally approval is automatic for public companies (save for administrative and clerical matters), except in cases of, say, shipping companies, where a declaration of nationality may be required. Since the duty to disclose on demand beneficial interests in the case of a company whose shares are listed on a recognized stock exchange applies only to members, a board of directors may insist on such disclosure on registration, but is apparently not entitled in law to insist upon it before allowing registration. In practice a hard-pressed board might well be able to insist on this information first. In the case of private companies a board of directors can usually refuse a registration, if they have some reason for doing so, because of the technicalities that are nearly always involved under the Articles of Association. Legal advice should be taken as to the exact manner in which the refusal should be minuted and notified to the shareholder concerned.

An alternative procedure may be followed on the death of a shareholder. Personal representatives to whom probate, or letters of administration, have been granted can, by a form of letter, request to be entered on the register in place of the dead shareholder. This letter is exempt from stamp duty, but the probate—or letters of administration—or an official copy must be lodged. In the case of a private company the directors may be entitled to refuse registration under the Articles. Usually the board can also call upon executors or administrators to apply for registration or transfer the share, but this depends upon what the Articles may say on the subject.

The payment of dividends

Dividends are payable to shareholders on the register. Until a transfer is registered the shareholder is entitled to the dividend and a purchaser cannot ask the directors to pay the dividend to him. So with large companies the right to close the register for a few days is exercised before a dividend is paid, to give time for the documents to be prepared for payment.

A shareholder can request a company in writing, using a form called a dividend mandate, to pay dividends to someone other than himself. Large companies have their own form for ease of administration, but the directors can act on authority in any form so long as they are satisfied it is genuine. Mandates are commonly used to arrange for dividends to go direct to banks, solicitors, or others who manage funds for their customers or clients. Mandates may relate only to dividends, and not to circulars or other documents which may still have to be sent to the addresses on the register.

Although the final dividend is a matter for approval by the shareholders at the annual general meeting of the company, when the accounts and reports of the directors and the auditors are considered, directors have a power to declare and pay interim dividends.

Dividends may only be paid out of realized profits and it follows that a company can only pay a dividend out of income if it has available profit that year. If there has been a loss rather than a profit, a dividend can be paid out of any surplus of past realized profits that have not so far been distributed or capitalized, so long as there is still a sufficient surplus after the loss for the current year has been deducted. If there is any fall in the value of all the fixed assets of the company, that has to be treated as a realized loss and reduces the profit available for dividend that year. If there is an increase in such value that is treated as unrealized profit and cannot be used as available for dividend or to pay up debentures or shares. Nevertheless a company authorized by its articles to apply unrealized profits in paying up shares in whole or in part by way of bonus may still do so. The only exception is in relation to fixed assets shown on revaluation to have been excessively depreciated under accountancy rules where the amount of such excess can be treated as a realized profit. In the case of public companies however, as part of the harmonization of Community law, an additional test must be satisfied. No dividend can be paid if the net assets are less than the total of the company's paid up share capital and the undistributable reserves. The definition of undistributable reserves covers items such as the share premium account, any surplus of unrealized profits or any other reserve which the company may be prohibited from distributing.

Directors should seek careful professional advice on distributions, on whether the company has made a profit or a loss. This is an extremely technical question now, particularly in relation to investment companies investing funds mainly in securities. These have additional tests to satisfy to show that their assets before and after the distribution will be 50 per cent more than their liabilities. This is complicated because companies do not normally provide for deferred taxation although, particularly with investment companies, this may affect ability to distribute and difficulties can also arise with foreign currency funding.

Capital dividends can only be paid out of capital profits, and if past income profits have been transferred to a capital account, they cannot be afterwards used to pay an income dividend. For the purpose of the rules governing dividends the only exceptions to distributions having to be made out of realized profits (except in the case of winding up) are bonus shares, redeemable preference shares redeemed out of the proceeds of a fresh issue of shares, the reduction of share capital by repaying shares or cancelling or reducing liability on partly paid shares.

The directors should concentrate on the question of whether the profit has been realized or the loss actually taken place, and if in doubt about this should consult their professional advisers. Again the question of solvency has to be considered because dividends must not be paid if the company is insolvent, that is to say, cash is not available to meet its commitments at the time payment is due, or sufficient cash would not be available to meet its commitments if the dividend was paid.

Limitations (intended to be temporary) in the past restricted the

profit margins of many businesses and the level of dividend of quoted
public companies. The way these worked in practice was different for
each company, but they no longer apply. In addition there is now a tax
concession in the treatment of increases of value of stock and work in
progress above a 1975 base figure. This means that a company may
have income profits, computed after taking such increases into
account, out of which dividends can be paid, but ought not to be paid,
because of the extra tax which would then be demanded. Directors
must treat this concession by the Inland Revenue with extreme
caution since it is liable to change once the Government has decided its
approach to the new Current Cost Accounting methods which might
replace the traditional historic cost method. In any event, if a company
reduces its stock and work in progress (so as to be more liquid at the
annual accounting date or to reduce its overdraft at the bank) the
Inland Revenue can claw back the tax forgone, since there has been a
realization. Nevertheless companies can, under professional advice,
transfer balances to reserves available for distribution as realized
profits which were provided originally to meet liabilities for taxation
which taxation was deferred and is not now likely to be paid.

Ordinary and preference shares

The right of shareholders to dividends depends on the terms of the
shares held by them. These commonly are either ordinary or
preference shares. The ordinary share, as its name implies, has no
special rights or disadvantages. It gives a right to the same dividend
that is paid on the other shares of the same kind or class. As a class,
ordinary shares are entitled to receive dividends declared in respect of
them and upon a winding-up to receive the surplus assets after all
share capital has been repaid. Companies may also have voteless
ordinary shares, frequently called 'A' ordinary shares. Holders are
usually entitled to all the same rights, except that of voting at general
meetings. Such shares are valued on the Stock Exchange at rather less,

because such shares carry no right to participate in the control of the company. The value of 'A' shares or the like is even less in a private company. The reason is that in a private company there are not the same practical sanctions and controls which apply in the case of a public company and which, because shares in public companies may be freely dealt in by anyone, are imposed for the protection of the public.

Preference shares, depending upon the precise terms of issue, usually confer a right to a fixed annual dividend out of profits available for dividend which may be paid once a year, or half-yearly or by other instalments, in priority to any dividend on the ordinary shares. The modern issues of preference shares have usually provided that the holders have no right to vote so long as the dividend is paid, and no right to participate in surplus assets after repayment of capital on a winding-up. The idea is that if the company gets into difficulty the preference shareholders should then be able to vote—and either seek to change the chairman and appoint new directors to strengthen the board, or to change the board completely. Preference shares may give additional rights; a right to receive a further dividend once ordinary shareholders have received a minimum, or to a special director appointed by them, or the right as a class to a veto, to prevent the company taking certain action such as exceeding its borrowing limits or disposing of its business.

Preference shares are commonly cumulative. If the directors are unable to recommend the payment of a dividend to them in any year either because there are no profits available, or because of a cash shortage, the preference shareholders do not lose that dividend. The company remains liable to pay them when it can afford to do so. Where the voting rights of preference shares are small the right of accumulation may be more important.

Deferred shares are sometimes created, which are the reverse of preference shares, because such shares get no dividend at all until the ordinary shareholders have had a minimum dividend. These usually carry votes, and more often than not are held by directors since the shares give rights to vote, while being cheaper to buy.

Loan stock

Changes in taxation have distorting effects on all company operations, so that issues of preference shares have been much less frequent with public companies, which do not have to answer to the Inland Revenue for their level of dividend, than in the case of private companies, where directors found that an issue of preference shares suited the family and domestic arrangements of their shareholders. Some institutional investors by virtue of the system of corporation tax are buyers of preference shares. However interest, payable on loans from directors, their families or trustees of settlements created by them, now qualifies as a deduction from profits on the calculation of the profits for the purpose of corporation tax. Most public companies, and a very few private companies that are owned by public companies, still find it cheaper to issue loan stock than preference shares. This is because interest is a charge on profits before corporation tax whereas dividends on preference shares have to be paid out of profits that have borne corporation tax—or at least treated as if they had. Companies having a foreign element which gives rise to debits or credits in making up accounts for tax purposes (whether to raise money with preference shares or loan stock) must realize that careful study with professional advisers is needed. The expression 'loan stock' is a convenient one to describe any arrangement under which a debt fund is set up and the units of that fund, in imitation of government stocks, are called stock. Such stock is usually transferable so that the original lenders can themselves raise money by the sale of it, and is repayable after a term of years, sometimes with a bonus or premium. The stock usually has a trustee who acts as administrator, keeps the transfer records, and is responsible for collecting or supervising the due collection of the interest and payment to the stock holders on the register, as well as the ultimate collection of the capital and repayment. The trustee may also have power to appoint a receiver for early collection in case of default or breach of conditions.

Private companies in distributing net realized profits can ignore net unrealized losses unlike public companies which have to deduct these in deciding to pay dividends. For this purpose interim accounts may be necessary.

There are frequently quite detailed conditions which the board has to see are observed in the conduct of the company's business, and for the holders of loan stock these are in effect policed by the trustee. As loan stock may not be attractive as an investment, boards of directors may have to consider giving stockholders a right to convert the whole or part of the stock into shares in the company at a price, probably rather more than the current price for the shares, or a right to subscribe independently for new shares. The attraction for such an arrangement, so far as the company is concerned, is that it may well help the company solve the problem of finding the money to repay the stock out of capital. On the other hand, it may well mean a shift in control away from the existing shareholders when the stock is converted into new shares. Directors should therefore consider most carefully any schemes for raising money by issues which are not going to be taken up by existing shareholders, because of the consequences that may flow from them. Careful independent advice is required in this respect, quite apart from that of merchant banks who promote schemes for fund raising on which they are paid by results. Such independent advice is also necessary on the conditions governing the issue of stock. Boards should be advised on such issues by their own independent advisers, for decisions of the directors may well affect drastically the interests of ordinary shareholders, as well as their own futures with the company, in ways they do not expect.

Charges on shares

A private company like a public company can borrow on the security of uncalled share capital, that is to say for the balance outstanding on share capital not yet paid up by the holders of the issued shares. However, private companies can enter into transactions in which the shares in the company are used as security. This occurs most commonly in connection with assistance to employees (not directors)

to take up shares in the company. This would include directors who
are or have been so employed but not directors who are or were
independent contractors. There is no special form for these schemes
so long as it encourages or helps holding by any of the classes or
persons included. Public companies whose business includes lending
money or hire purchase or the like can take security on fully paid
shares in connection with a transaction in the ordinary course of
business. Changes in existence are not invalidated by the new rules
under the 1980 Act when a company registers or re-registers as a
public company.

General prohibition on finance for shares

Directors must not permit a company to provide financial assistance to
anyone to acquire shares in their company or a holding company, even
in the case of an unlimited company. Whilst the penalty in the past was
minor this has now been made a serious offence and directors must
avoid giving any direct or indirect assistance whether by loan
guarantee or provision of security. In any event the provision must not
have the effect of reducing the net assets of the company or, if it does,
can only come out of profits available for dividend. There is an
exception for companies whose business includes the lending of
money. Loans to bona fide employees (other than directors) with a
view to their purchasing or subscribing for fully paid shares for their
own benefit are allowed. Similarly companies may provide money in
accordance with an employee share scheme for the time being in
operation for fully paid shares to be purchased or subscribed for by
trustees. An employee share scheme is now defined as a scheme for
encouraging or facilitating the holding of shares or debentures in a
company by or for the benefit of bona fide employees or former
employees of the company, its holding company or other group
companies and includes spouses, widows, widowers and children
(including step-children) under the age of eighteen.

Chapter 3

A company's officers

The managing director is a special creation of the Articles of Association, and is really a sub-committee of one director to run the business of the company and report to the board. In the nineteenth century boards of directors of public companies tended to be supervisory in character, and no executive employees were allowed to sit on the board at all. This system, heavily criticized as autocratic and undemocratic, was retained at least by some insurance companies and banks until recent years. The system puts a heavy burden on the chairman and the other directors to attend sub-committee meetings of the board and to make business and commercial decisions. It led to the concept of the managing director rather than the executive or managing committee. Under the Articles a managing director, who is an employee on contract to act as such, is usually empowered, so far as all persons dealing with the company are concerned, to make any contract or decision without the authority of a board resolution. He can, in practice and in law, seal documents acting jointly with the company secretary, who is usually under his executive control, without reference to the board. The fact that company secretaries have to have a level of qualification for this office and so carry responsibility for compliance with all statutory duties, may well mean that the company secretary will tend to be less under such control. Indeed liaison between executive officers and the board of directors should be improved by this change of emphasis.

At one time, the signatures of two directors were necessary in law so far as a purchaser was concerned, and some Articles still provide for this. Common caution dictates that there should be an agreed basis of internal consultation, and that the managing director will make only certain types of decision without approval of the board as a whole. It is interesting to note that on the Continent a different division has been developed between the supervising board, whose members may not be members of the executive management, and the functionary board, which runs the business rather like a managing directorship in committee. The present law is sufficiently flexible to allow companies to be organized on this basis.

It is possible for a company to have more than one managing director, or for there to be deputy managing directors or other fulltime executive directors, such as a finance or property director. The division of functions must depend on the board, but as far as people dealing with the company are concerned any managing director can commit the company completely. It is not safe to assume this in the case of a deputy managing or other executive director without getting legal advice as to the effect of the Articles of the particular company.

The legal approach to this follows common sense, although the permutation of events in human affairs can produce peculiar results in particular cases. The rule is that where a company has been publicly constituted by statute or by registration, the people dealing with the company are bound by what its documents say, whether or not they have read them or had a report from an adviser. But there the obligation stops, and such people are entitled to assume that the management is being properly run and continue doing business, unless they have been warned to the contrary. If a loan is therefore made to a company in good faith, but the consent of the shareholders should have been obtained first, it is not in law the responsibility of the lender to see if that consent has in fact been obtained. Lenders, as a matter of commercial caution, will normally check up to see if such a consent is necessary, but this is a matter of prudence. The loan can be made and any other business done on the signature of the managing director alone. All that is necessary is to see that the managing director may have power to do what he is setting out to do; but the other person must act in good faith, and if he knows that a consent is necessary and also knows it has not been obtained, he is not protected by the rule. This is the reason for the commercial caution, when directors are dealing with other companies in transactions which are not the daily business of those companies, in getting their advisers to make a search in the official records of these companies, to see if there are any special conditions or peculiarities relating to the powers of the managing director, or indeed of the board of directors as such.

A managing director may be appointed to hold office from year to year, at a salary, or for a fixed term, or indefinitely, or subject to notice like any other employee; but a person dealing with the company can deal with a person he believes to be a managing director as long as the company behaves as if this is the case.

The chairman

The chairman of the board under most Articles is appointed by the board, and both the chairman and the managing director can only hold their offices whilst they are directors. The chairman, by virtue of his appointment, is also the chairman of the shareholders' meetings. He presides at meetings, and by law the minutes of the meeting, if signed by him, are presumed to be a correct record of the meeting until the contrary is proved. A chairman does not need the approval of anyone to authenticate the minutes although it is customary either to circulate the minutes or to read them out at the next meeting, and only then to sign them. It is also possible for the chairman of the next succeeding meeting to sign. This rule applies not only to meetings of directors and of shareholders, but also to meetings of committees.

The main function of the chairman is to preside at meetings, and if the chairman himself is not present or leaves the meeting, any director present can take over. The directors present have to settle who should preside among themselves, and commonly there is some protocol laid down by the board minutes, with a director being named as the vice- or deputy-chairman. Some companies allow the managing director to fulfil this function, if the managing director is not already chairman. Others avoid this, on the principle that the chairman's function is to supervise management and not be part of it.

The chairman's duty is to keep order and see that business is properly conducted. In the absence of formal standing orders to regulate meetings, apart from the rules as to the form in which resolutions are to be put on the agenda and decided, the proceedings are very much in the hands of the chairman, who tends to follow traditional debating procedures. This is in fact the practical legal requirement, which is that meetings should be conducted so that views of shareholders may be properly heard. There is a presumption that the decisions of the chairman on points of order and incidental questions are correct, and his decision is usually said in the Articles to be conclusive as to whether a person has a valid vote, or whether a proxy vote is valid. Except in the case of special or extraordinary resolutions where a poll is demanded, a declaration by the chairman is conclusive evidence that a resolution has been carried, but only if the declaration does show it was passed by the proper majority. On the show of hands a poll can still be demanded formally, and the chairman must declare the result in accordance with the poll. The chairman must accept that the meeting continues during the taking of the poll, and cannot close the poll or the meeting until voting is concluded, although he may adjourn it for the voting to take place on a subsequent day. A chairman can even arrange for a postal vote if he considers it to be the fair procedure. In any event either the chairman or the meeting can appoint scrutineers.

The Articles usually give the chairman a casting vote, except in the case of some private companies which are divided between two or more groups, and in which it is intended that in cases of equality there should be a deadlock position or some arrangement for decisions by an outside umpire or arbitrator. In such cases, as in a partnership, provision is usually made that resolutions fail automatically if not agreed.

The chairman, or some other members of the board according to ordinary practice, may propose resolutions, and these are then put by the chairman to the meeting for discussion. It is the chairman who supervises the questions to be resolved and who later authenticates the minutes prepared by the secretary. For this reason, where private copies of resolutions are required by the Companies Registry, such copies are signed by the chairman. When extracts of minutes are required, for example as instructions to operate accounts by banks, it is requested that they should be signed as correct extracts from the minute book by the chairman and the secretary. It is for the same reason, namely his power of authentication of authority, that many people in commerce prefer to correspond or communicate with the chairman on important or unusual business, particularly if there is no managing director.

Associate and alternate directors

In modern commerce, many businesses, to impress their customers, confer the status of a director upon an executive who is not to have the full status of a managing director. This can make the boards of large businesses too cumbersome, or can involve the executive in matters, beyond the purely commercial aspects, in which for one reason or another it is not intended that he should be involved. For this reason, the concept of the associate director has been devised. Such a person is usually a department head or manager by another name. It is entirely the creation of the Articles under which the associate director is appointed. Usually he attends board meetings by invitation only, does not have the general rights of a director of access to all aspects of the business of the company, and is given little or no special right to represent the company in such a way as to bind it. Commonly it is a courtesy title, but it does indicate that the status of the individual is such that he may be called in by the board to voice an expert or practical opinion. Curiously, such a person is not a director for the purpose of the Companies Acts, but most companies will mention his name in a return filed with the Registry, who will accept it. On the other hand, he may incur the liabilities of a director if in fact he acts as one. Similarly a person appointed as an associate or alternate director should comply with the rules applying to directors that require notification of interests in shares or debentures of the company and associated companies.

An alternate director similarly is not an appointment to the board of directors, but a temporary delegation. Such an appointment can only be made if allowed by the Articles, and it is to permit someone to attend meetings of directors in place of a director himself, if for any reason he is absent. The alternate normally has to be another director—who therefore has two votes—or a person approved by the other directors. He is appointed by a letter from the director he represents which gives notice of his appointment, and his removal is by the same method, or by resignation. The alternate director's appointment also ceases to have effect if the director ceases to hold office for any reason.

A director who fails to attend board meetings, depending on the Articles, may be removed from office, and the power to send an alternate may therefore be of great advantage. It is also useful when there are divided interests represented in a board room and an absentee would mean that one side lost voting strength. The alternate director will not be entitled to the remuneration of the director, but must look to the director, who, depending on the Articles, would be responsible for the actions of the alternate, for his pay and expenses. It may be that the alternate will have to have a share qualification as well as the director. The register of directors should record the appointment and removal of an alternate, and a return must be made to the Companies Registry, as for a change of director. Alternates usually speak and vote, and an alternate must make a disclosure of any personal interest in any matter being dealt with by the board in the same way as a director.

The company secretary

The secretary of a company is appointed by the board under the Articles, and particulars of his appointment and removal have to be recorded in a separate register from that of directors, but for the purpose of returns to the Companies Registry the same form is used for both directors and secretary. A company can appoint more than one secretary or other officer and can divide their duties. Public companies commonly appoint a registrar to keep the membership records, but only the office of secretary has to be named in the Register and notified to the Companies Registry under the Acts. Companies may appoint a deputy secretary, or sealing clerk, so as to have an alternative available. The appointment of a deputy secretary or of an assistant secretary has to be notified to the Registry.

It is the duty of the directors of a public company to take all reasonable steps to secure that the secretary or each joint secretary (but apparently not a deputy or assistant secretary or a sealing clerk) is a person who appears to have the requisite knowledge and experience to discharge his functions. If he already held such an appointment, a secretary can continue but on new appointments he must have held such an office for three out of the last five years. Otherwise the board must be satisfied that the candidate holds or has held some other responsible position or that he has a professional qualification such as being an admitted solicitor or a called barrister or advocate in any part of the United Kingdom or that he is a qualified accountant or chartered secretary or member of some other body the directors consider appropriate.

The statutory functions of secretary are substantially the same for public and private companies, the only real difference in duties being that with private companies the secretary has to sign the annual returns recording compliance with the requirements for a private company. Although the actual direct statutory references to the functions of secretary as distinct from references to officers generally are comparatively few, the secretary has to deal with most of the official administrative work. This has led to a separate professional

organization, known now as the Institute of Chartered Secretaries and
Administrators. The Institute has its own qualifying examination, and
publishes its own *Manual on Secretarial Practice,* which is a highly
technical production, the first edition of which appeared in 1912 and
which is regularly brought up to date.

The strict duties of the secretary really fall into four parts: (i) the
preparation of the agenda for meetings, attendance at meetings and
preparing the draft minutes for the chairman; (ii) arrangements for
statements of stock at the end of each financial year and for
stocktaking; (iii) statutory and other duties in relation to the
convening of meetings and formal matters in connection with them;
(iv) provision for accounting records which have now to be kept up
with entries day by day of all moneys received and of assets and
liabilities. In addition to these strict duties company secretaries
frequently undertake other matters of daily routine administration
and also deal with Stock Exchange requirements. While it is for the
directors to decide whether the accounting records are to be kept at the
registered office or elsewhere, these are now to be available for
inspection by the officers of the company. Before the 1976 Act the
right of inspection was limited to directors. This statutory right of
access for the secretary is therefore significant. Knowledge brings
responsibility, and the right of the secretary to inspect tends to change
his status in relation to finance directors and group accountants. This
is the case particularly with public companies who now have to have
someone of professional status to perform this office.

The secretary has to send out the notices and proxy forms at the
right times for the nature of the business, see that the resolutions are
circulated and also any other documents that ought to go to the
shareholders. This means in turn the supervision of such details as the
preparation of envelopes in which to send out the circulars, and
preparing memoranda for the directors as to who should move and
speak upon resolutions. A secretary will also prepare notes to assist the
chairman, including matters that might be mentioned in addition to
those on the agenda. The secretary will book the room and arrange the
seating. He should not only see that the auditors are represented when

appropriate, but also the company's solicitors in case the chairman is faced with sudden technical problems, as can always happen at shareholders' meetings. The secretary has to check the proxies to report to the chairman for his decision, and must have available for inspection at the meeting records of the directors' share interests and other information which shareholders are entitled to see. Finally, he has to organize the filing and circulation of documents consequent upon the meeting, in particular sending extracts to officers or senior managers concerned, and perhaps attend to press releases and notices to the Stock Exchange. All of these activities, if the company's affairs are in any way involved or contentious, can produce traps for the unwary, but it is the board, and in particular the chairman or managing director, who will have to answer for them in public, because all of the activities involved are supposed to be under the supervision of one or other of them. Nevertheless the secretary should always be vigilant to see proper procedures are followed, and that the board is not acting in a manner contrary to the authority conferred upon them by shareholders through the Memorandum and Articles of Association. This is even more important now that companies are no longer protected by the rule that acts beyond their powers were invalid even if the other party involved acted in good faith.

If the company goes into liquidation or a receiver is appointed, the secretary can be called upon to answer questions as an officer of the company, and a receiver has the right to call upon the secretary to countersign the statement of affairs by directors.

With public companies having a quotation on the Stock Exchange there are further detailed requirements to be followed for the sake of orderly marketing, and here again the actual conduct of these matters is usually the concern of the company secretary.

With the small private company the position is in practice very different, as the entire company may only be two people. There is a rule that a sole director cannot be the secretary as well, but if there are two directors one can be the secretary. It is possible for a company to act as secretary to another company. It should be mentioned that a sole director cannot have as secretary a limited company of which he is the

sole director! Many accountants organize special companies to
provide secretarial services rather than use an individual employee.
This also avoids the problem that partners or staff in a firm of
accountants, who are the auditors to a company, must not work for
that company, for example as secretary.

The secretary, under the new provisions penalizing persons for
default in making returns under the Companies Acts, appears to be
liable to disqualification from taking part in the management of a
company. In the case of professional secretaries, particularly of public
companies, or organizations providing secretarial services this is
perhaps more severe as a penalty than it would be for an executive or a
controlling shareholder director, who is primarily concerned in the
business enterprise for his livelihood. Directors must therefore expect
and be prepared to be sympathetic to pressure from secretaries to
comply with official requirements.

The company seal

The seal of the company, which has to be fixed or impressed on those
documents which are to operate as deeds, is selected by the board of
directors after incorporation. The seal contains the full name of the
company and sometimes a design. In practice, a specimen impression
is included in the minute book against the formal resolution adopting
the seal as the common seal of the company. For a seal to be used
validly, the statutory provisions require the sealing to be witnessed by
a director and the secretary, or by a second director or some person
appointed by the directors for this purpose. Where a document only
requires to be authenticated it is sufficient for it to be signed by a
director, secretary or other person appointed for this purpose, and the
seal does not have to be used. However, a person other than a director
or secretary, who is to be given this power, ought to be appointed as an
assistant secretary, so that the appointment can be filed at the
Companies Registry for official reference. Otherwise it may be
necessary to seek authentication from the director or secretary of that

person's authority to authenticate! The seal is commonly kept at the registered office, and it is the responsibility of the secretary to see that it is in a secure place. At one time it was the practice for special padlocks to be inserted in the press in which the seal was mounted, so that it could only be unlocked for use by the secretary and a director, each with his own key. A company can also have a Securities seal, in addition to the common seal, which is a duplicate with the addition of the word 'Securities' on the face. This can be used for shares or warrants.

The auditors

The auditors of a company are a special statutory creation. Strange as it may seem, before 1900 there was no special rule for auditors to be appointed and carry out a periodical audit. The statutory requirement for an audit has provided a firm and broad basis for accountancy practice. It has also provided a self-supervising system which has enabled government taxation to operate at a level and to such an extent that the State is in effect a partner or joint proprietor of every company incorporated to carry on business. The first auditors have to be appointed by the board and must be qualified accountants of proper standing, who are not unfit as a result of statutory restrictions. Once appointed, auditors stay in office from the conclusion of one annual general meeting to the conclusion of the next. This cannot be concluded until the accounts, together with the reports of the directors and the auditors, have been prepared and laid before the meeting. If no auditors are appointed or re-appointed at a general meeting at which the auditors have completed their duties for the previous year, the Minister can appoint. Notice has to be given to the Minister by the board within one week of such meeting that his power has become exercisable. It is possible for the board to appoint the first auditors at any time before the first general meeting at which the audited accounts are to be presented. The board also has power to fill a casual vacancy, amplifying the power of the company in general meeting. The auditors are to be elected each year afresh, and the retiring auditors are not now re-elected automatically without any resolution. Apart from this, since 18 April 1977 a company can by ordinary resolution remove an auditor before the expiry of his term of office, but there are strict rules as to the procedure, on which legal advice should be taken if removal is thought to be desirable.

The auditor can be an individual or a partnership firm, but not an incorporated company. One particular snag about changing the auditor is that, in order to propose that he should not be re-elected, it is necessary to give twenty-eight days' notice to the company, yet the notice to convene the meeting is twenty-one days'. This means it is always too late for a shareholder, who objects at the annual general meeting to the way the annual accounts appear or the auditor's comments on them, to take action that year. The board, or a member of it, can give formal notice to the secretary at the registered office, because they will have seen the auditor's report before the meeting is arranged. It is usual to send out the accounts and the notice at the same time.

Any resolution dealing with a change of auditor has to be the subject of twenty-eight days' previous notice to the company, which has to pass a copy to the auditor being appointed or replaced. The auditor can provide a statement which has to be sent with the notice of the meeting to the members or, if too late, has to be read at the meeting. The court can restrain a statement on application if the rights are being abused to secure needless publicity of defamatory matters. The outgoing auditor is entitled to notices and to attend any meeting which concerns him as a former auditor. Auditors also have a special right to resign by notice, but this is not effective unless it sets out the circumstances connected with their resignation which ought to be brought to the attention of members or creditors, or states there are none. A copy has to go to the registrar within fourteen days and, if it sets out such circumstances, to everyone entitled to notices of meetings. There is the same right within the fourteen days for the company to apply to court to restrain the further issue of a statement as needless publicity for defamatory matters. Apart from this, if the notice does contain a statement, the auditor can requisition a meeting to receive an explanation. The auditor can also provide a detailed statement to accompany the notices calling the meeting, or if this is not available in time, have it read out at the meeting. There are matching provisions for subsidiary companies.

It is also now a criminal offence to make a misleading, false or deceptive statement to an auditor.

Directors are responsible for seeing that the auditors are properly qualified. At one time this was not necessary, but new auditors of companies with a quotation on the Stock Exchange, or subsidiaries of such companies, must now be members of one of the recognized professional bodies, which are the Chartered Accountants' Institutes of England and Wales, Scotland and Ireland, and the Association of Certified Accountants. There is power for the Department of Trade to add or delete bodies. Foreign accountants such as the French *commissaires aux comptes* are not acceptable to the Stock Exchange as auditors. For other companies, a person could be qualified if he was specially authorized by the Department of Trade as a result of a qualification or experience received in the course of his employment with a qualified firm or outside the United Kingdom and had a certificate from the Department to prove it by virtue of experience in the United Kingdom. No one may act as an auditor if he is an officer or employee of the company or its group, or is a partner of such a person. A consultant to the firm of auditors may be a director, and this may not disqualify the firm. Up to 1971 there were exceptions which arose from transitional provisions of the 1967 Act. Directors, particularly of private companies, should be careful to check the status of their auditors. If an unqualified auditor has been appointed, it is a nullity, and the Department of Trade will have to appoint another auditor.

The auditors are entitled to receive notices or circulars as if they were members, and to be heard by the board and by its members in any matter which concerns them as auditors. The auditors are not merely required to report to the shareholders on accounts examined by them and on the balance sheets for the general meetings, but also to make statements about various matters such as the terms of employment of directors, or alternatively see that this information is set out in the directors' report, or in notes which form part of the published accounts.

The accountancy profession has taken many years to produce and publish standard systems of audit practice. These are affected, somewhat, by the extent to which Parliament has imposed its own regulations upon the profession and the standards seem to have been evolved primarily for large corporations which are audited by the major firms of accountants. Small private companies will probably evolve practical responses to matters raised by these standards and auditors will no doubt be flexible since, in the ordinary way, their institutes are unlikely to invoke disciplinary proceedings. The main sanction is the possibility of a negligence claim against auditors if the report should have been qualified and someone succeeds in a damage claim because the auditor was lax compared to the published standards.

The directors have to recognize the specific duty of the auditors, and must provide proper access and facilities to enable the auditors to form an opinion on whether proper books of account have been kept, and proper returns adequate for audit purposes have been received from branches not visited by the auditors. They must also be able to report whether the balance sheet and the profit and loss account of the company, or consolidated profit and loss account, are in agreement with the books of account and official returns. It is the essence of the procedure that, in reporting to the shareholders, the auditors are stating that in their opinion a true and fair view is given. In the case of the balance sheet this will be of the state of the company's affairs as at the end of the financial year, and similarly in the case of the profit and loss account, unless it is a consolidated account of the company's profit or loss for the financial year. If the accounts are consolidated accounts by a holding company for a group, then the opinion relates to the state of affairs and the profit or loss of the company and of its subsidiaries as dealt with in the accounts. It is the responsibility of the directors and not of the auditors to value stock. Directors, as a matter of audit practice, are asked to certify these values. Indeed, the balance sheet and accounts are supposed to be drawn up by the directors and presented to the auditors. In one sense this safeguard procedure as envisaged by Parliament has been reduced to futility, because although auditors may not be employed by the company, it seems that this nevertheless allows them to give their professional services as accountants. The result is that, with many small private companies, the accountants not only prepare the accounts but keep the books as well. In the case of larger companies or firms trading under the same name or an associated group practice, they advise on such companies' business, administer stock and other control systems, and may, through an associated firm, provide management consultants for the company. The result is that the auditors prepare the accounts in draft for the directors to approve. Unless directors are in dispute, or in difficulty concerning some item over which they cannot agree a compromise formula with the auditors for treatment on the accounts, nothing adverse is usually disclosed in practice in the report.

The auditor may act as the accountant to the company in whole or in part. In theory a company should have its own accountant, head of its counting house or cashier, who prepares the statements and accounts not only for the shareholders, but also for the other participator in the business, the State. Books of accounts have to be kept and all tax returns made, not merely in relation to Corporation Tax on the profits of the company, but also in respect of tax deducted from wages, National Insurance contributions, Value Added Tax, and all other imposts and duties for which the company has to account to the Inland Revenue or the Customs and Excise. Once again the auditors are called upon to assist or execute much if not all of this work where the company secretary does not have the ability to undertake this or to head a department which does it. Directors are generally well advised not to try to carry out much more than the routine work. Their professional advisers have specialized knowledge or skills, or know-how to make them available at reasonable cost, so as to minimize properly and within the law the amounts which have to be paid in one form or another to the State, and to arrange the cash funding to provide the payments.

It may well be in time that those who provide accounting, taxation and other advisory services, will not be allowed by law to also act as auditors. For the present, however, directors are able to and should make full use of the range of services available to their company through their own professional advisers. It is now the policy of the professional institutes that an auditor should not be a shareholder of a company in which he holds office as auditor.

Auditors, directors, company secretaries and other officers have a special right to be excused from liability for their negligence, default, breach of duty or trust if they have acted honestly and reasonably and the court considers, having regard to all the circumstances, including appointment, they ought fairly to be excused. In such a case the court may relieve them from liability in whole or in part. Further, anyone who thinks a claim may be made can apply for relief in anticipation. This provision is not dissimilar to the provisions of the Trustee Act 1925 which gives trustees relief in such circumstances. It helps to explain why, apart from other technical factors, it is difficult for a shareholder to recover damages against auditors who fail to comment on circumstances likely to involve the company in economic disaster if not taken in hand. This is not to say that there are not combinations of circumstances in which a shareholder can and will succeed, but it makes settlement more attractive than litigation when dealing with auditors.

Chapter 4

Buying and selling

Every sale and purchase by the company, or by its director or agents for the company, is in civil law the responsibility of the company alone. Neither the directors nor shareholders have any rights or obligations if goods are bad or faulty, unless there is actual dishonesty or such gross carelessness or recklessness that it is indistinguishable from dishonesty. In such cases the person who is physically responsible for the events will be personally liable jointly with the company. Claims of this kind are normally actions for tort. This is a classification which has been the subject of much argument among academicians as to its accuracy. It means those cases where the English courts would recognize that the events proved in court show that the person concerned has suffered injury or damage, and that the person who caused injury or damage did not behave as a responsible citizen and should therefore pay compensation.

As has been mentioned, when a deal (which is outside its legal trade) is done in the name of the company, this gives the customer the choice of suing either the person with whom the business is done, or the company, but not both.

Since a limited liability company has only the assets made up from cash or other property provided by the shareholders in exchange for their shares, the money it has borrowed, plus the profits of its trade and such grants as the State may allow, credit for its trade has to be watched very carefully. No matter how distinguished the shareholders may be, a creditor has no claim on them beyond the amount which it is their obligation to pay for the nominal share capital issued to them. Once money or value is given for the shares issued, that is the end of the matter. In 1972, the Treasury thought fit to issue a statement on this very point. Although the Government may have a financial interest in a company, whether as minority, majority or sole shareholder, this in no way operates as a guarantee of the company's solvency, nor are the creditors in any way indemnified against the normal commercial risks of doing business with such a company. Of course there are cases where the Government undertakes or has undertaken a specific commitment in relation to those debts. It may be reasonable to take a commercial view that, because of damage to his or its reputation, or unfavourable reaction in other spheres of activities, a substantial shareholder or associate of a company will come to the rescue and avoid the scandal of failure and insolvency. Indeed, many leading companies regard it as a positive advantage to have the reputation that they would not allow the collapse of a company with which they are identified as major shareholders. Where there may have been such inferences or suggestions, it may in some circumstances be possible to sue a major shareholder, if one is disappointed by the collapse of a company. In such cases there is a real prospect that a shareholder who cares for his reputation will choose to make a compromise settlement out of court. Nevertheless, unless the distinguished associate gave a guarantee or undertaking, in law the associate has no liability. One important factor is that public companies may find it embarrassing in relation to their Stock Exchange quotation not to meet the liabilities of their subsidiaries, but this does not really assist the creditor.

In company transactions three factors have therefore to be considered:

(a) with whom the business has actually been done. Many large companies use different companies for group purposes, with goods ordered on the letterhead of one company, Paper Products Ltd, acknowledged by a second company, Confusion Products Western Ltd, and payment received by letter enclosing a cheque from a third company, Confusion Products Head Office Ltd. A repeat order may then be sent in another name, Confusion PP International Ltd, again paid for by a different company. Just to compound this, it is common to find that, with the use of computerized accounting, different code numbers are assigned by the computer operator to the various companies, or that they are all simply put into one account, Confusion Products. No man of commerce really has time to sort this out, and when trouble comes, as it so often does, the lawyers are left with a sticky mess. That is their job. The problem for the man of commerce is to prove which company got credit; it could be the wrong one! It is therefore essential to establish, in correspondence, with which company business is being done. This will presumably be the one for which satisfactory references have been received or trade enquiries made! The order confirmations, invoices and receipts going to that company must be kept;

(b) whether the company is creditworthy. It must be watched continually for fundamental changes in organization which may affect this. Change can occur in various ways, for example by the issue of a debenture to a bank, or to some other money credit source. This has the effect of giving the bank, in case of insolvency, the right to claim title to all assets, and the proceeds of them, in priority to other creditors. In particular, it may mean that a manufacturer who has delivered goods to the insolvent company cannot take them back and cancel the debt even though sold under a contract under which title is reserved until payment was made; and

(c) whether to insist upon personal guarantees of the account, from the principal directors or shareholders. This has the effect of getting round the general principle of limited liability.

Guarantees are most frequently sought by landlords in granting leases, or permissions for leases to be assigned to private companies, and by banks or other finance sources such as hire-purchase companies. The request for a guarantee of a trade account by suppliers is less frequent, particularly with small accounts, but it should always be considered.

The agreements and contracts of companies are generally made in the same way as those of individuals, except that, where the agreement is in writing, it must be signed by a director or other authorized officer. Where the agreement has to be a deed under seal, such as a lease or mortgage, then the company must seal it. Normally, a company does not seal an agreement unless the document is intended to operate as a deed.

The operation of bank accounts

Bank accounts have to be the subject of special arrangements for the company, since the banks have to establish not only that the company has power to operate a bank account, but also how the operation is authorized. The penalty for failure to check these matters is the risk of losing the right to repayment. For this reason banks require to see the Memorandum and Articles to check if there are any special features of the company in its constitution. Banks also require to see formal resolutions passed by the Board stating precisely who may sign or endorse cheques and bills of exchange, and who may give instructions on which the Bank may act with impunity. The evidence of these resolutions is in the form of a copy certified by a director, usually the chairman, and by the secretary to be a true copy. The banks make printed forms available on demand to customers, and there is little difficulty in completing such resolutions, including an authority to allow overdrafts. Commonly in such cases, if a new company wishes overdraft facilities, the bank will press the directors to give a personal guarantee of any credit allowed to the company, or to give collateral security.

A cheque is a type of bill of exchange, but a company may also give ordinary bills of exchange. A bill of exchange is usually an instruction by the drawer to another person, who owes or has agreed to make money available, to pay that money to a third party, because the third party has purchased the right from the drawer. For many centuries this has been a method of money payments between traders and others, particularly on an international basis. The order has to state a time when payment has to be made by the person on whom the bill is drawn. The time can be on demand, by production or presentation of the bill, on a fixed date, or after a period of time, such as ninety days. The bill should also state whether it is to be paid only to the third party, or to the third party or as he shall order, or even simply to the bearer. The person on whom the bill is drawn is not bound by it, unless he accepts the bill, which is usually arranged so as to justify the third party purchasing the bill. Once accepted, the acceptor is liable in the same way as the drawer of the bill. Bills can be endorsed with an instruction by the third party holding the bill to pay someone else, usually as the result of a sub-sale of the bill at a discount. If a person who has properly bought and paid for a bill is not paid when he presents it, the bill is dishonoured. The holder can then sue the person who endorsed the bill, unless it was sold on the basis that this endorsement was without recourse— *sans recours*—and that these words were written on the bill as part of the endorsement. Another form of negotiable instrument is the promissory note, which is simply a promise to pay a debt created for value. This commercial IOU can be endorsed over to a third party, in the same way as a bill of exchange, by the person entitled to the benefit signing a direction to pay it to the third party.

A company can give any of these instructions, either by sealing the bill or by having the same signed on its behalf by a director or other authorized officer of the company, but it is essential that the person signing should do so in a way that makes it clear he is signing for the company, and give its correct name. Signature by directors of bills is a highly technical procedure and it is as well to take legal advice to ensure that what is done does not make the director personally liable where this is not intended. Furthermore, he must have authority

under the Memorandum and Articles to sign. Anyone can be
authorized, but it is as well to see, as banks do, a certified copy of the
resolution of the board which gives authority to such person to sign,
unless he is the managing director. It is sufficient for a company, and
may perhaps be commercially convenient, to seal instead of having a
single officer sign on its behalf.

Guarantees

Negotiable instruments start simply as the means of passing debts.
They are used not only between traders, but also between various
finance institutions, as a means of transferring credits instead of using
currency or bullion which are thus needed only to settle the
differences between active institutions on national or international
scales. At the same time negotiable instruments are also used to
provide finance for traders, as a means of providing credit. For
example, a company may be asked to give a banker's order, which is
drawn to operate as a promissory note. This can then be used by the
lender to finance his own company. In addition, a director may be
asked to join as a party and to 'back' or endorse a promissory note or
bill as a form of guarantee, but this in practice will make the director
liable as a principal and not merely as a guarantor.

As a result of the new legislation on loss relief for Capital Gains Tax,
a parent company may be better off guaranteeing a loan to a subsidiary
by a third party, say the bank, than lending the money direct so long as
the guarantee is given after 11 April 1978.

It should be appreciated that a guarantee is only a promise to pay if
the debtor does not. By law, a guarantee must be by agreement in
writing. It is also a rule that, if the lender departs from the terms of the
debt agreement, the guarantor is not liable, but it is usual to provide in
contracts of guarantee that time for payment of the debt allowed to the
debtor, or other forbearance shown to the debtor, will not release the
guarantor. When the agreement is of a running account a guarantor
can always give notice to stop the guarantee running, but he remains

liable for the reducing balance on the account from the date the notice
becomes effective until the final amount is paid off. Directors who
give guarantees should appreciate that, if called upon to pay, they take
over the rights of the debtor against the company. In the case of a
hire-purchase agreement this means the directors can claim the
equipment. If it is a mortgage or debenture, the directors are entitled
to the priority in respect of the assets charged by it which that gives
against other creditors, so long as they stipulate that payment is made
by them as guarantors.

For guarantees given after 11 April 1978, directors may also be
entitled to claim an allowable loss for Capital Gains Tax if called upon
to make a payment but the rules as to qualifying loans are complex and
advice should be taken. It is particularly important in this respect for
directors to replace old guarantees which will not carry such an
allowance if a liability arises.

Directors' loans to the company

Directors frequently make loans to their companies, particularly if
they are also shareholders, either by paying money to the company or
by not drawing salary or commissions to which they are entitled.
These loans rank equally for commercial purposes with all other loans.
Despite this, directors of insolvent companies will be pressed by the
other creditors to stand back on moral grounds and let the other
creditors be paid first. Directors are entitled to interest, and as long as
this is at a fair commercial rate it will be allowed as a deduction from
the company's profits for tax purposes. If directors' loans are repaid,
directors must be sure that the company can meet its other
commitments when they fall due, and not appear to be preferring
themselves to other creditors, particularly if the company is in
financial difficulty. Directors who are shareholders have also to be
careful about money lent by them to start the company in business,
since the repayment of a first business loan may be treated by the
Inland Revenue as a dividend attracting income tax, including tax at

higher rates, which was previously known as surtax. Furthermore, repayment of directors' loans may in any event enable the Inland Revenue to argue that the company could have paid larger dividends instead, and so claim additional taxation.

There is a further aspect to consider regarding Capital Gains Tax. A loan account lost because a company fails or is sold off at a loss may produce an allowable loss that can be set off as a deduction from any future capital gains but the rules for allowance are complicated. The rules are different for loans made prior to 11 April 1978 so that directors should rearrange their loans to take account of this. Money put in by way of share capital, perhaps as preference shares, does give rise to an allowance in case of a loss. The question as to the way money should be put into a company therefore requires careful consideration at the time with professional advisers, even though the director is making a loan to his own company.

Sources of funds

A company has basically seven sources to provide funds for its activities apart from internal finance out of profits. These are:

(a) hire purchase and leasing of equipment;
(b) loans privately negotiated;
(c) the placing of shares or debentures;
(d) factoring, which is the sale of trade debts owed to the company at a discount;
(e) bills of exchange which are commonly for payment in 90 or 180 days;
(f) long-term trade credits with a supplier on special business terms; and
(g) government grants.

Whether all or any are appropriate for the business of any particular company is a matter for professional advice.

Finance and merchant banks

It is better in some cases to arrange for a private company to start in business with a loan from a bank; most directors will find little or no difficulty about dealing with a simple bank advance from the local branch of one of the big joint stock banks.

Merchant banks also act as a source of loans, but these institutions should more correctly be regarded as finance operators, having their origins with merchants or dealers who used their expertise in business generally. Such bodies do not simply lend money; they help other businesses to raise money from investors and from the public, who are often willing to put up money because the merchant bank is associated with the enterprise. A merchant bank is also assumed to be jealous of its own reputation, and so will have investigated the situation of the company seeking to raise money and will be well informed about it. The various types of City of London finance institutions have in recent years tended to merge and to join in groups with the merchant banks; indeed, many new banks were launched, while others became so distressed as to require life-boat assistance organized by the Bank of England, and some have even sunk completely. This has led to new codes of conduct on the part of banks, finance houses and deposit taking institutions under the general supervision of the Bank of England as the central Bank.

These merchant banking organizations tend to be conglomerate advisers and seek to recruit accountants, brokers and lawyers into the firms themselves. Directors must exercise caution in dealing with merchant banks and should seek the guidance of their company's own accountants and solicitors on business transactions with such banks. Indeed, reputable merchant banks will insist upon this. On the other hand, City finance business tends to be highly specialized and directors may find themselves encouraged to appoint new accountants or solicitors for the purpose of dealing with the transaction in hand.

Directors should consider this carefully, since while the solicitors and accountants acting for the merchant banks or for the issue provide the expertise, the solicitors and accountants who have dealt with the company hitherto may be the persons best able to see that the documents are correct and to advise on the new commitments involved.

Public finance corporations

Associated with merchant banks but independent of them are public finance corporations like the Estate Duty Investment Trust (EDITH), the Industrial and Commercial Finance Corporation (ICFC), the Finance Corporation for Industry (FCI), and the so-called 'nurseries' of the merchant banks. These provide loan capital for private companies which have not reached the size, importance and stability to justify an offer of shares to the public, but which can sometimes be in serious difficulties, perhaps because a major shareholder has died and death duties have to be paid, because a new development programme has to be financed, or even because sales are running at too high a level. All of these organisations may provide funding in one way or another and the return they require will vary with the state of the market. Commonly, the demand will be for participation in the equity, that is to say the chance to take and own a part of the business. Conditions will be imposed as to who will make up the board of directors, the terms of service agreements, control of the business, and even as to borrowing from other sources. The effects of these arrangements can be far-reaching in their implications for the future of the business. It is for this reason that directors should not allow their own business judgment to be confused by the displays of financial expertise. It has been said that merchant banks are like expert sailors who will see the ship through any storms, battle with all the problems, but are nevertheless likely to sell out to the highest bidder on the basis that it is always right to make a profit, even if this involves making the directors walk the plank on the way! It follows that excellent business results can come from working with merchant banks, but that one's guard should never be relaxed.

Mortgages, debentures and loan stock

There are three basic forms of loan documents for companies, apart from negotiable instruments, hire-purchase and credit sale arrangements. They are the mortgage, the debenture and unsecured loan stock.

Strictly a mortgage is a charge on an asset, usually land, although any asset can be mortgaged. It involves giving to a lender, as a security for his loan, the prior right to sell the asset for his own benefit if the debt is not repaid. It is of the essence of the arrangement that the mortgaged property remains the property of the borrower, who continues to enjoy the use of it and merely hands over documents of title to the lender. This must be distinguished from a pledge or pawn, when the thing mortgaged is handed over to the lender to be kept locked up until the money is repaid, with a right to sell if it is not repaid.

The expression' debenture' under the Companies Acts in fact includes a mortgage, but in common use it can be a 'floating charge', or a fixed and floating charge. By a floating charge debenture a company commits its assets to the lender on the basis that if at any time default is made in observing the conditions of the loan the debenture holder can appoint a receiver and manager, who can sell the assets which the company owns at that time and, subject to payments which have to be made in priority, use the proceeds to repay the loan. This floating charge only operates or crystallizes when the default takes place. Accordingly, debentures may also include a fixed charge, a mortgage on a particular asset such as the business premises of the borrower, with which there can be no dealings without the consent of the lender. In the ordinary way fixed charges have not been created in

respect of stock in trade or plant or equipment, because sufficient
security was given by the floating charge. However, if goods are
supplied, in accordance with recent developments in the law, on the
basis that title does not pass until the supplier is paid then a receiver
and manager can do nothing but return them. If the supply is of raw
materials which become incorporated into a product before the
supplier is paid however, it seems that the right to trace and claim back
the raw material in its new form would be inoperative. A fixed charge
defeats title retention and it may be that the use of such fixed charges
or debentures will be extended. Meanwhile directors of companies
giving and taking credit will need to take advice from solicitors on
their terms of business and whether or not their terms of business and
whether or not they are free to give meaningful floating charges or can
rely on them.

Unsecured loan stock, on the other hand, does not give any priority
of security on assets. It is usually an arrangement in the form of a trust
deed under which a trustee is appointed to see that the company obeys
the rules laid down as to the way it should conduct business, and to see
the money is repaid at the end of the period of the loan. If it fails to
keep within the financial conditions for the running of its business, the
trustee can appoint a receiver and manager to take over and run the
business, and can at least in theory sell the business whilst there are
still sufficient assets left in the company to be sold to repay the loan
stock. As loan stock creditors do not take priority over trade creditors,
and may even be deferred to them, this type of loan is more acceptable
for companies which require substantial credit from suppliers, or who
in the course of their trade hold the property or commodities of
customers for work or processing. Since 1965, because of corporation
tax, many companies switched from preference shares, whose fixed
dividends have to be paid out of profits on which corporation tax has
been paid, to loan stock, because interest on loan stock is a deduction
from the profits before corporation tax is payable. Again, because
finance sources like to participate in the improving profits earned,
convertible loan stock has been developed as previously mentioned. It
is of the essence of the arrangement that these loan stocks are capable

of being sold; and in settling the details directors should seek specific commitments, and not mere statements of intention which cannot be enforced. The people with whom the directors have to deal in the future may well be different from those to whom their confidence was given in the first place.

Loan stock trust-deeds usually contain a series of rules affecting the way the business may be conducted. These are intended, among other things, to restrict the amount which the directors may cause the company to borrow. These provisions have to be studied very carefully, particularly where a company has foreign loans which have to be repaid in their original currency. Companies have suddenly found that, as a result of changes in exchange rates, the debt limits, expressed in sterling or other currency terms, have been exceeded because the cost of repayment was so much more than the amount originally borrowed. This aspect must be closely watched, and professional advice taken to ensure that the company has so arranged its affairs as to anticipate and provide for changes in margins.

Chapter 5

The company abroad

Abolition of exchange control

Whilst English, Welsh and Scottish companies have always been
engaged in international trade beyond the United Kingdom, much of
the business has been conducted within limits imposed by exchange
control. These limits in various ways affected the manner of business
for many years. All except the oldest directors (that is to say those who
might well need a resolution to re-elect them because they are over
seventy) have little executive experience of working without these
restraints. Further there have been such changes in taxation that the
impulse to conduct business abroad has also changed.

In the first instance companies no longer have to remit foreign
currency profits back to the United Kingdom for conversion into
sterling. It is perfectly possible for a company to keep and maintain
foreign bank accounts without permission, except that of the foreign
government, if required by their law. Equally it is possible to maintain
bank accounts in England in currency other than sterling. Even
comparatively small companies may be able to save the expense of
conversion of funds in and out of sterling by this means and cheques
may be issued in a foreign currency. There is a cash flow trap,

however, for the unwary. It may take many weeks to clear a foreign cheque paid into an English bank account, so that if payment is to be made from abroad by cheque the company secretary should perhaps organize a local foreign bank account.

One more trap for the unwary board of directors is to be found in Third World Countries who may not easily permit payment to be transmitted out of their country if the money is paid into a local account. It may be that the opening of such an account will be treated as establishing a branch liable to local taxation. Distinctions between capital and income remittance may be found to exist. It has even been known for samples of machinery once landed not to be allowed out again although no local buyer has been found. Finally the caution must be uttered that currencies, like commodities, are liable to sudden and unexpected deterioration. Arbitrage, the business of dealing in currencies, has its own experts who earn their money by their expertise. It may be that a company would be better-off accepting the expense which is the price of minimizing the risks. In particular this can be done by buying or selling currency in advance of payments as a form of insurance which is now available.

Setting up

Another area which requires consideration and advice is the decision to set up business in a Community or foreign country. In this respect, whilst the abolition of exchange control is a restoration of liberty, it also means that directors no longer have to satisfy the Bank of England that the venture is sensible and viable, likely to comply with the official standards of investment return in terms of capital and income. Many companies may have been frustrated, but many others were grateful that there was this critical review by the Bank whose staff had a great deal of expertise about local conditions. There was also a very pragmatic view about funding the difference between the official and unofficial price that might have to be paid whilst the necessary provision of gratuities for local officials was also well understood.

Directors should, in making such decisions, bear in mind these matters. They ought to make sure, before venturing into a new foreign locality, that the topics which had to be reviewed for permission to capitalize foreign operations of any scale are reviewed and made the subject of a comprehensive written report. It can be surprising when this is done how different the project may look, even to the writer. Advice is desirable as to whether it is better to conduct the business on behalf of the company in its own name or through a separate subsidiary company. Not because of tax, but because of local exchange control or other restriction, it might be as well to consider whether to operate in a subsidiary incorporated locally, or in the United Kingdom or in some other country. In addition the trading subsidiary may be owned by another company incorporated in the United Kingdom so as to be free, in spite of local regulations, if it is necessary to sell the United Kingdom company (and the foreign operation it represents) to a buyer without local tax, licensing or exchange control or similar problems. It is also important for boards to take legal advice not only on the tax implications, but on all the local law which involves matters such as employment and product liability as well as freedom of movement of assets. Study of the stepping stones from one country to another should take place at the time a start is made when it need not be expensive, particularly if advice can be taken by the United Kingdom lawyers from local lawyers. If left to a later stage, the dimensions and difficulties may undermine the viability of the operation.

It is also important to decide upon the local advisers whose opinions are sought. There are international firms who have a grasp of the problems of starting up between one particular country and another. On the other hand the use of local foreign advisers, in correspondence with United Kingdom advisers who know the business of the company and are aware of its problems and the priorities of the board can be more advantageous. This is particularly the case where, as happens in many foreign countries, international firms are restricted and all sorts of assistance in guidance and introductions may be more readily available from a local firm. Again in setting up any such foreign operation care must be taken to ensure that the appropriate work permits and visas are obtained, because these may be required for say English members of a foreign subsidiary, even if they do not reside in that country. The alternative may well be that it is necessary to have a board made up of at least a majority of local residents, so as to make the company responsive to local laws and pressures. Another complication is the development in some parts of the United States (and elsewhere) of taxation, not on profits made by the subsidiary or branch locally, but as a proportion of the group profits as a whole. This developed from the practice of moving goods within the group so as to leave the local company with a small profit margin.

Taxation and duties

There is legislation in many countries to regulate accounting for tax and customs duty purposes, but it is difficult to enforce. The approach of taxing upon the basis of the group's international profit is in many ways simpler to enforce. This is a cause for considerable concern if profits earnt in the country are low, particularly because it takes time to build up a business in a new country. It may lead to a decision not to trade as a group of interlocking companies, but instead to do business with companies that are owned and controlled locally. In such cases the profit is taken in terms of fees or royalties on agreements under which knowledge and experience are made available ('know-how'), or even trade marks, copyright or patent licences, perhaps coupled with some form of sole distributorship for the products or components for the products from the United Kingdom. Directors should take advice upon the various legal alternative methods available to them.

Another equally important consideration in arrangements for foreign trade is whether the foreign tax concessions match with the United Kingdom corporation tax. It may be that the local law allows that until the capital cost is recouped there is no local tax—this encourages investment. On the other hand the profits may still be regarded as trading profit liable to corporation tax back in England.

Conversely, if the capital is later realized (which would not be taxed in the United Kingdom unless there was a gain) it may be taxed as trading profit locally. Often agreements are made between governments of countries which trade with each other to try to avoid both governments taking full tax on the same profit. It is realized that in such cases, either business would be stopped or the parties driven into evasion and illegality. Accordingly there are double taxation conventions which are designed to reduce the mischief. Naturally the agreements usually work on the basis that the taxpayers have to pay on the higher rate as between the two countries, but it is better than paying twice. Good accounting advice can be most important in this respect.

Foreign contracts and arbitrations

Directors must always remember that business transactions can go wrong and it is vital to ensure that any foreign agreement complies in all respects with the local law, quite apart from the Community law rules on competition. The document should not only comply with the formalities, which may include a requirement that it be recorded by a public notary but also state the law of which country is to govern it. It should also state whether the parties agree to submit any disputes to the courts of the country whose law has been chosen or whether these should go to arbitration, and if so what arbitration. This is of particular importance where the local courts may not be impartial or where the contract is with a State agency or trading corporation. Directors are usually well aware of trade association arbitrations, but unless they are using a standard contract which commits the parties to an expert trade arbitration for their trade, this can be overlooked. It may well be that it is then necessary to get the other side to agree to arbitration, something which may not always be possible. Sorting out a dispute in accordance with its merits can prove extravagantly expensive or unduly prolix if these matters are not dealt with in the original documentation. Indeed directors and company secretaries may well find that omission of these terms from foreign trade agreements by oversight, and not for good reason, is precisely the sort of conduct which can expose them to claims by dissatisfied shareholders. Whilst preparation of these clauses or other clauses may be the responsibility of the legal adviser, if he is asked to draw the contract, directors commonly conclude negotiations before the lawyer is involved—if he is involved at all.

Breaches of foreign law

Mention has also been made elsewhere of the potential liability of directors under foreign local law. Much depends in this respect not just on whether the director is liable to come before the local court, but whether the country in question has a judgments convention with the United Kingdom, so that awards for civil damages in local courts will be enforced by a United Kingdom court.

It must not be thought, in the ordinary way, that directors are likely to have an unfair foreign judgment enforced against them back in this country. On the other hand such claims can be made and the recent judgments convention with the United States in particular makes this remote possibility seem a little less remote.

Chapter 6

The annual report and accounts

It is a fundamental condition of incorporation that a company shall keep proper books of account. The records must be kept so that they will give a true and fair view of its state of affairs and explain its transactions. This means that there must be recorded receipts and payments, sales and purchases, assets and liabilities. The requirements for the keeping of accounting records were revised in 1976, and the new regulations apply as from 1 October 1977. These have to be sufficient to show and explain the company's transactions. A director has to make sure that the accounting records show, with reasonable accuracy, the financial position of the company at any time. In addition, they are supposed to ensure that any balance sheet or profit and loss account prepared by them complies with the requirement to give a true and a fair view. Accordingly entries are to be made in the accounting records daily of all moneys received and expended by the company, and the matters in respect of which the receipt and expenditure takes place. It is important to note that on the face of it the convenient practice of many small businesses of writing up the books once a week may be a technical offence. Apart from this directors have to make sure that the records contain the assets and liabilities of the company. Where the company trades or deals in goods the statement of stock at the year end, and all statements from which it was prepared, must show the goods and the buyers and sellers in sufficient detail to be identified, except in the case of goods sold by way of ordinary retail trade. There is no definition of 'ordinary retail sale' and it remains to be seen how this will be understood by the courts. The accounting records must enable the directors to produce accounts in accordance with the statutory obligation to give a true and fair view of the company's state of affairs and of its profit or loss primarily in relation to cost.

The records do not have to be in bound books, and can take the form of loose-leaf ledgers, card systems or the more sophisticated mechanical or electronic systems. These methods must be such that ordinary reproduction in legible form can be made if required. Further it is not sufficient to keep only up to audit. The records of public companies must be kept for six years and those of private companies for three years, although directors would be well advised to keep them for six years. The court on winding up can order preservation for longer periods. It is the duty of every director and other officer, not only to see that such records are properly kept, but also that adequate precautions are taken to guard against falsification and to facilitate the discovery of fraud. Failure to see that this is observed renders directors liable to prosecution and to default fines, although a director can escape liability if he thought that a competent and reliable person had been employed to attend to this. In this respect the responsibility can be passed to the company secretary. Equally, directors are entitled at all times to have access to the company's premises to inspect these records. If records are kept outside Great Britain periodic accounts and returns must be sent at least every six months to an office located in Great Britain. These must disclose the financial position with reasonable accuracy, and contain enough information for the annual accounts to be prepared.

The company secretary and the auditors of the company are entitled to access to the records at all times and to require such explanations as they think necessary; this right of inspection, like that of the directors, includes all statutory registers and the minute book.

It must be appreciated that Parliament's approach to records has changed over the years. Originally, these were to be kept for internal use to show how, in the case of insolvency, a company given the privilege of incorporation had conducted its affairs, and for the shareholders to be satisfied at all times that their moneys were dealt with properly. Now the State has a direct interest in the business of all companies, by virtue of the many kinds of taxes which companies have to pay. In addition, in order to direct and control the economy, the State requires information which can enable it to compile national statistics and returns. Aside from this, because of the changes in monetary values and the effect of complex taxation, shareholders want more information about current values and current trade as well as forecasts and estimates of future business. There are complaints that the accounts are out of date by the time of publication and are far too complicated. This underlines the problem of trying to give too much information, with all the delay this can cause in preparation.

Whilst some companies compete to produce the most interesting and informative reports and accounts, others do no more than the minimum to comply with the law. The problem is that disclosure may prove damaging to the undertaking either because it assists competitors or because it may cause suppliers or customers to change the basis of trade or unions to question policy. This is particularly the problem with international trade and foreign governments. Directors must weigh all these factors and may well have to exercise restraint when dealing with auditors and seek legal advice. There has to be a continuing dialogue between Government and the various interests.

Annual report and accounts

Apart from the keeping of records, which shareholders are not allowed to inspect, the board must produce an annual report and accounts.

There are elaborate statutory requirements as to what should be disclosed by the report and accounts and this presents formidable problems for members of the board of a large company where the directors and shareholders are not closely associated with one another. In theory, the report should be prepared by the secretary, working in association with the company's chief accountant. Frequently the secretary will be professionally qualified, and will perform both functions. In most small companies a firm of chartered accountants or suitably qualified accountant acts as an auditor and will prepare both the report and accounts, since the secretary is either an employee or a director who doubles in this capacity, and who may have little or no knowledge of the technicalities.

At this point it is convenient to comment that the story of the board that kept three sets of accounts, one for the Inland Revenue, one for the shareholders and the third set for the board, is no longer apocryphal. There is little doubt that the accounts in the form of statutory returns for the Inland Revenue frequently present positions different from those disclosed by the accounts to the shareholders. The Inland Revenue see both, the shareholders do not. Until recently the creditors of many private companies saw neither! Management accounts, particularly for the purpose of controlling cash flow, make up the third set. Even the published accounts of public companies used to be able to conceal secret reserves. Much of this has now been changed. The accounts of all limited companies must be published by filing a copy with the annual return at Companies House, made up to an accounting date which has to be notified to Companies House during the currency of the year. The right to maintain secrecy of profits has now been abolished for all except a few banking and shipping companies; the big joint stock banks have been coming over to the practice of full disclosure of profits. The 1967 Act did allow those who valued secrecy to convert their company into one without limited liability by a statutory procedure, since companies without limited liability—and which are not owned by limited liability companies—are exempt from this requirement to file accounts.

The fact that companies have had to publish turnover figures and export figures under the 1967 Act provided data for the Government

to make the change to Value Added Tax. It became possible to
dispense with the requirement for turnover to be stated when it is less
than £250,000 per annum. Each company, in common with all other
businesses, provides direct to the Inland Revenue the special forms
containing returns of turnover on which tax is based. At this point it
should be noted that these forms, with their statutory penalties for
incorrect statements, are most useful for calculation and checking of
payments under agreements as to royalties and licence fees. The Act
also provides the basic machinery for the collection of rents based on
turnover, for shops and similar premises. It is possible for rents
intended to be geared to turnover, which is an American practice, to
utilize these returns as the basis for calculation.

Directors have to decide the period of the financial year for their
company. This must not vary by more than seven days either way
from the date of which notice has been given to the Companies
Registry, although the 'year' may be between fifty and fifty-four
weeks. The board can at any time during a financial year give notice
specifying a date in the calendar year to which the accounts will be
made up, so as to extend or shorten the period. A period cannot now
be for more than eighteen months. Further, except in the case of
alterations within a group of companies designed to make accounting
periods coincide, it is not possible to give notice altering the year end
date after the year has expired. Directors will no longer be able to
come to a conclusion about changing a financial year end after the
accountants have prepared provisional figures because it will be too
late. It will therefore be advisable for the board to draft provisional
accounts, probably based on monthly management figures, towards
the end of the year (or to call on their accountants earlier for this
purpose), so as to have the relevant information to make a change in
time. Furthermore, in the ordinary way the period is not to be
extended more than once in five years—there is no such restriction on
shortening. Legal advice should be taken when changes are in
contemplation.

For new companies their first accounting period must be not less
than six or more than eighteen months. All companies in existence

have to give notice specifying the date in the next calendar year to which their accounts will be made up. This notice is only to be given six months after incorporation or the operative date, which was 1 October 1977. If not, a company is fixed with 31 March unless the Registrar of Companies will agree some other date for it. Clearly this is a point to watch as a most dangerous tax trap.

Accounts have to be laid before the company and delivered to Companies House within ten months of the year end, or seven months if it is a private company. There are means of adjusting these crude provisions for business outside the United Kingdom, the Channel Islands and the Isle of Man but the problem is that accounts will have to be dealt with much more quickly than has been business practice in the past. This will mean that both the Board and the Inland Revenue will have to work with approximate figures and estimates to avoid accounts being delayed until actual figures can be known.

Transitional provisions dealt with the filing of an annual return in the old form for periods before 1 October 1977. Appropriate meeting provisions are made for group accounts and special obligations have now been introduced for overseas companies to prepare and deliver accounts. This responsibility is something which will affect in particular anyone who is a director of such a company in the United Kingdom. In this case the obligation is not just to deliver copies of the relevant balance sheet, account or document, but to provide a certified English translation unless an English version is prepared. Overseas companies are liable to make returns from the date when a place of business is or was established in Great Britain. These changes were made because the Registrar of Companies was concerned with the failure of companies to file on time under the old regulations and the difficulty of enforcing the old provisions.

The rule is that the annual accounts and report, which are primarily intended for consideration at the annual general meeting of the shareholders with a report by the directors, must be filed at Companies House so as to be available for public reference. These ought to be sent for filing at the same time as they are laid before the shareholders and in the same form. The company has to make separate

statutory tax returns for various purposes, with which such reports
and accounts are supposed to be consistent, but these are not normally
disclosed or included with the report and accounts sent to the
shareholders. The fact is that the contents of annual reports and
accounts are directed and dictated by statute rather than by the
Articles of Association of the company. Their preparation requires
skilled and professional assistance for all but the simplest and smallest
companies. While there is no obligation on directors for their report to
be scrutinized by the auditors, it is nevertheless advisable because of
the complicated particulars which may have to be given. Directors
may be personally liable for inaccurate or misleading information in
these reports. It would be as well to have the various details and
information checked and certified to the board by the company's
auditors, or by the company's solicitor, and also confirmed in writing
by the individual directors or the senior employees concerned, as may
be appropriate. It should be noted on the other hand that accountants
now frequently ask the directors to confirm the accuracy of the
material upon which the audit is based. If nothing else, it is a salutary
reminder to the board of its general accounting duty and it could, in
certain circumstances, shift responsibility in negligence from the
accountant to the directors personally. Directors should not sign such
certificates or letters of representation at the request of auditors
without a formal confirmation in return. This confirmation should
accept responsibility in so far as the extraction of the material, or
indeed the keeping of records and accounts, has been undertaken
either by staff from the auditor's firm or from some other firm of
accountants and that the work has been carried out properly and all
relevant matters brought to the attention of the directors for the
purpose of the directors giving of such a certificate. It would be quite
unfair, having paid substantial fees for the work to be done
professionally, for the responsibility to be shifted to the directors by
the use of such certificates.

    The report, with the accounts, has to be circulated not less
than twenty-one days before the date of the annual general
meeting to:

(a) every member of the company, whether or not he is entitled to receive notices of meetings of the company;

(b) every holder of a debenture of the company, whether or not he is similarly entitled; and

(c) other people entitled to receive it.

The annual return has to be filed at Companies House within forty-two days after the annual general meeting.

Obviously there is a time lapse before accounts become public knowledge in the case of private companies, but companies quoted on a stock exchange have to arrange to release full particulars to the Stock Exchange and the Press at the time the report and accounts are posted. This invariably means that the professional operators always have this information before it reaches the ordinary shareholder in such companies. It also means that the accounts become public knowledge before they are approved by the shareholders, for whom they purport to have been prepared.

The fact that the accounts are usually out of date is an additional problem. This probably does not matter where the company is a small company, in which all the shares are in the hands of the directors or their intimate associates. The problem is that the larger and more diverse the company or group of companies, the more difficult it is to prepare the report and accounts for a year on a true and fair basis, because events are never static. The balance sheet and the profit and loss account have to be made up at the end of the financial year. This must be a date not more than ten months before the date of the meeting of the company (or seven months if it is a private company). If the company has interests abroad, outside the United Kingdom, the Channel Islands and the Isle of Man, notice may be given of this fact claiming a three months' extension. The first accounts, apart from complying with accounting dates' time scales, have to be laid before a general meeting not later than eighteen months after incorporation, and after that at least once in every calendar year. The Department of Trade has power to extend these periods. Companies which do not trade for profit can produce an income and expenditure account, instead of a profit and loss account, with the balance sheet.

The balance sheet must give a true and fair view of the state of affairs of the company on the date to which it refers, and the profit and loss account a like view of the profit and loss. The accounts have to comply with the requirements of the Eighth Schedule of the Companies Act 1948, as amended. Where the company has subsidiaries, the profit and loss account can be framed as a consolidated profit and loss account, dealing with all or any of the subsidiaries as well as the company, so long as it complies with the requirements of the Act relating to consolidated profit and loss accounts, and shows how much of the consolidated profit or loss for the year is dealt with in the accounts of the company. Accounts should also be based on the same standards and criteria each year, and if in a subsequent year some different method is used, this should be disclosed. Without consistency there can be no meaningful comparison of one year with the next.

The accounts have to disclose particulars of substantial property or non-cash transactions, of loans and finance to directors and connected persons (but in the case of recognized banks only the aggregate amount) as well as the aggregate amounts of loans and finance in favour of the company secretary and other officers. If the accounts or group accounts fail to set out information the auditors, so far as they are reasonably able to do so, have to put this in their report.

The Institutes of Chartered Accountants and Certified Accountants, in adopting a whole series of accounting standards to which companies now have to adhere to obtain unqualified auditors' reports from such accountants, are trying to secure greater uniformity. This is considered socially necessary in view of the ever-increasing balance-sheet sophistry produced by the desire to pay the minimum of tax whilst presenting the maximum financial probity. The Stock Exchange, for quoted public companies, require additional topics to be dealt with, in particular an explanation as to the reasons for adopting an alternate basis of accounting. The Government has powers under the Health and Safety at Work etc. Act 1974 to require inclusion in the annual report of information for securing health, safety and welfare at work of employees and protecting others connected with the employees' activities against risks to health or safety. In addition the Government has power to demand information that does not appear in the report so as to be available to shareholders. Many companies are now introducing an annual circular for employees to explain the actual results of trading as well as to provide other information, and copies of these circulars are sent to the shareholders with the annual report. This would appear to be a sensible approach and to provide a method which can be developed to meet the need for more social information about the larger companies, which is the underlying trend.

Group accounts do not have to be produced where the company is itself a subsidiary of another British company, and directors can always decide to leave out a subsidiary for reasons permitted by the Act. Group accounts laid before a holding company can consist of a consolidated balance sheet and a consolidated profit and loss account, and these may be wholly or partly incorporated in the company's own balance sheet and accounts. Furthermore, if the directors consider it preferable, the accounts do not have to be fully consolidated if the group accounts may be readily appreciated by the members in some other way, so long as the same or equivalent information is presented. On the other hand, a combination of the listing agreement for quoted companies and the accounting standards adopted by auditors require the consolidation in group accounts of the proportionate results of associated companies if there is a holding of 20 per cent or more of the equity share capital, where the company owning the shares participates in management or is otherwise involved more than an ordinary investor would be. This has been criticized because, in the absence of special agreement or articles, profits of a company in which less than a majority of the shares is owned are not disposable profits and are not available for distribution by the company owning the shares to its own members.

Directors can take advantage of these broad general provisions to ensure that accounts mask some hard information which would be of use to competitors, critical shareholders or the wage negotiator on

behalf of the company's employees. However, the professional bodies
controlling the accountants' profession have been seeking without
direct legal authority to adopt rules to produce even more uniform
practices and treatment. These may well become obligatory.
Directors should therefore follow these recommended practices as a
general rule. Opinions do vary among accountants over the changes
and the extent to which the standards should apply. Directors should
take care to ensure that all advice by auditors in relation to practices to
be followed in respect of company accounts are fully and clearly
recorded in writing. One requirement is in respect of accounting for
inflation which may produce very different figures, particularly in
relation to cost of sales and depreciation items. The result will suggest
that profits are less than those shown by the historic cost method. This
in turn, in view of the new requirements for companies in defining
what profits are available for distribution must lead to controversy.
The better view seems to be that the historic cost accounts are the ones
upon which decisions must be made in law and that current cost
accounting is merely management information from which to judge
the commercial wisdom of any action. If directors wish to present only
current cost accounts without the authority of the shareholders these
could be rejected. Such a change of practice ought perhaps to be
authorized by special resolution since it is possible to argue that for the
directors to change the conventions is a constitutional change which
needs the authority of such a resolution. Since the Inland Revenue
require accounts for taxation on the historic cost basis, which have to
be approved by the shareholders to be the accounts for taxation
purposes, the point may not arise. Current cost accounts are less
factual than historic cost accounts because a whole series of
assumptions and estimates have to be made on current replacement
expenses of stock and equipment which cannot readily be checked.
Further, these assumptions may be quite unrealistic in that
depreciation is charged on items which may have a useful life far
beyond that allowed in the calculations. In this context the proposals
for depreciating building costs required under the new standards leads

to the solemn farce of producing a figure which has no regard for the underlying, real value. This is required even though buildings on land in this country (where building standards are extremely high and planning laws restrictive) are much more substantial and in fact have tended to increase in value at rates greater annually than the proposed depreciation. Again, depreciation so charged is not allowed as a charge against profits before taxation by the Inland Revenue. It must be appreciated, however, that it is envisaged that these standards will be used in the context of companies trading internationally where very different considerations apply. Directors should therefore take legal advice as to the presentation of their accounts if they are unhappy with the auditor's proposals or possible qualifications on the auditor's report.

For the same reason, the 1967 Act imposed new requirements for the inclusion in the directors' report of information that did not appear in the accounts. Further embarrassment was caused when it was found, following a series of take-over bids of large companies, that well-known firms of accountants were passing accounts and giving unqualified reports when the real situations were completely different, with the result that the published profit figures were misleading. On the one hand, a successful bidder for a profit-making rival would find that, when the rival's accounts were prepared by his own staff, using his own firm's methods of valuing and stock, the rival was in reality losing money. On the other hand a skilful operator, following a take-over bid, could re-arrange the accounting procedures with the result that substantial profits would be engendered for the next two or three years. This 'proved' dynamic management, and enabled the operator to use the high value placed on his own holding company, because it could achieve 'growth', to take over more companies on which the operations could be repeated.

The new accountancy standards may make this more difficult in the end, but for the next few years the confusion caused by so many companies changing over to a new accounting system will provide many opportunities for such operations. Directors and shareholders should not, in dealing with accounts in any bid situation, rely on the published accounts in order to make comparisons with their own company for this reason alone, without expert guidance.

The directors' report is generally signed by the secretary on the authority of the board, unless the balance sheet has to be signed by two directors. The report must set out the amount of money which directors decide should be paid by way of dividend, and the amount to be carried to reserve. It will also usually state which directors have retired or are due to retire by rotation at the meeting and, if eligible, whether they are offering themselves for re-election. Directors should check this carefully with the company secretary or accountants as a mistake can mean losing the office of director. Similarly, where a director reaches seventy, care must be taken to see that special notice is given. In addition, the report will disclose whether the auditors are intended, if eligible, to continue in office. Their remuneration for the year is commonly left to the board to fix, although shareholders can resolve how much should be paid. This is one of the historic anomalous practices which remains unchanged. It would be in order for shareholders to fix the auditors' fee at £1 instead of trying to pass a resolution that the auditors be not elected! No doubt the accountants could still claim for accountancy services, but in practice, unless there were exceptional circumstances, there would be a change of auditors following such a resolution.

Disclosure requirements

The report may refer in general terms to the company affairs, but must now disclose the following:

(a) *General matters*

(i) the names of the persons who at the end of the financial year were directors of the company, and changes during the year with dates. This is historic, since it deals with the position at the end of the year which will always be different from the date of the meeting; and

(ii) the principal activities of the company and of its subsidiaries in the course of that year, and any significant changes in those activities during the year.

(b) Fixed assets

If market values differ substantially from what appears on the balance sheet, those differences, which the directors—not the auditors—consider to be of such significance as to require the attention of the members or debenture holders, are to be given with such degree of precision as is practicable.

(c) Issues

If the company has issued any shares or debentures, the reason for making the issue must be given, with particulars of what has been issued and what the company received.

(d) Contracts

Contracts in which a director is interested. This always applied if the directors considered a contract was of significance in relation to the business and that the interest of the director in the contract was material. It applied to an interest which existed at any time during the financial year. It does not apply to a service agreement which has to be referred to a meeting if it is to be for more than five years in any event. Nor does it apply to other matters which relate to the director or persons connected with him which have to appear or be noted in the accounts. These take in transactions involving substantial property or non-cash assets which the company has acquired or disposed of and loans or finance given or allowed. The mere fact that a director is simply a director of the other party to the contract does not make it a matter for disclosure in the report, even if it makes that company a connected person for a substantial property transaction or loan reference in the accounts.

(e) Schemes

Schemes to promote shareholdings by directors. This applies when the company is party to an arrangement to enable directors to acquire

benefits through obtaining shares or debentures in the company or
any other company.

(f) Directors' interests

Directors' interests in shares or debentures. A special register has to
be kept and this information has to be extracted and summarized. It
must include not only holdings in the company but also any subsidiary
or holding company. The figures must be given both for the beginning
and the end of the year. The interests of spouses and infant children
must also be stated. Directors must give notice of their dealings with
shares or debentures within five days—before 18 April 1977 this
period was fourteen days. If the security is quoted the company must
give notice of such a dealing to the relevant stock exchange before
close of business the next day (leaving out of account Saturdays,
Sundays and Bank Holidays).

(g) Material particulars

Material particulars for an appreciation of the state of the company's
affairs disclosure of which is not harmful to the company or its
subsidiaries in the opinion of the directors.

(h) Turnover and profitability

This does not have to be given when turnover totals less than £250,000
in any financial year. When it has to be given, the turnover figure
should appear, together with the method by which it is computed, in
the profit and loss account or by a note annexed to this account so that
the turnover figure is subject to the auditors' report. If the company
has during the year carried on two or more classes of business, except
banking or a similar activity, there has to be an explanation in the
directors' report. It is for the directors to decide what are the classes of
business. The directors must also state their opinion as to the extent to
which each class of business contributed to the profit or loss of the
company before taxation. Where there are group accounts, the
statement as to contribution to profit relates to the group position.
Classes of business which do not differ substantially can be treated as
one class.

(i) *Particulars of employees*

This applies where the total number is one hundred or more. At the end of each financial year the directors' report has to contain a statement of the average number of employees and the aggregate gross remuneration, including bonuses paid or payable. Benefits in kind are to be omitted. This is to be calculated on the average number employed by the company in each week of the year, no matter how short the hours worked in the week by the individual employee, and the aggregate paid or payable to such persons for the year. A holding company has to publish one set of figures for the group. Each subsidiary, if it employs the required number, has to give these particulars in a report relating to that company. Employees wholly or mainly working outside the United Kingdom are to be disregarded. There are peculiar factors to be taken into account. A person employed by more than one company ought to be treated as one. Part-time cleaning staff are included, but not contractors. A person ill or absent on holiday is still to be counted. Employees on strike would not be counted. Common sense suggests that this will give rise to unreliable figures, since a cleaner working for five employers in a week will count as five people in any national employment totals!

(j) *Contributions for political and charitable purposes*

This does not catch donations in kind or the provisions of services, but only money payments. If during the year a total of more than fifty pounds has been given for charitable or political purposes, the directors' report must disclose the payment for such purposes. The reports of partially owned subsidiaries have to disclose donations, but reports of wholly owned subsidiaries may omit these. The directors of all holding companies must treat donations by the group as a whole and must report accordingly.

When a donation for political purposes is made for more than fifty pounds, the person to whom the money has been given must be named, or if the donation or subscription is to a political party the identity of the party must be disclosed, and in either case the specific amount must be stated. Money is treated as given for political

purposes if directly or indirectly a company gives a donation to a
political party of the United Kingdom or any part of it. This includes
gifts to separate constituency parties. The definition also treats
donations as being given to a person who at the time is carrying on, or
proposing to carry on, any activities which reasonably can be regarded
as likely to affect public support for such a party. This is intended to
catch organizations which, while not directly engaged in political
activities, in fact foster the aims of one or other of the parties. The
wording in practice catches almost any sort of organization concerned
with politics. There must be knowledge that the person is carrying on
such activities and if directors omit the statement on a donation in all
innocence this is an acceptable excuse. A donation to a foreign political
party is not deemed to be for political purposes. Once reported, it is
for the shareholders to approve or disapprove of the conduct of the
directors in making such donations. In general terms donations of this
character do not seem to give rise to controversy in shareholders'
meetings, perhaps because the amounts involved are usually
insignificant in relation to the affairs of the company as a whole. A
shareholder might claim that a political donation was outside the
powers given to the company by its Memorandum. The problem then
is to show that the donation, if not expressly authorized, is reasonably
incidental to the business of the company, where, for example, the
donation was solicited by some influential customer or associate,
whose custom or goodwill is of some importance, or by some employee
whose willingness to serve the company may be concerned.

Where the donation is for charitable purposes, gifts to persons
ordinarily resident outside the United Kingdom do not have to be
reported, and detailed particulars do not have to be given of donations
to a particular charity, only the amount of the money. The charity
must be exclusively charitable; for Scotland, this is defined in relation
to the Income Tax Acts. It is likely that a gift for charitable purposes
will be within the powers given to the company by its Memorandum,
but it must be borne in mind that although there is a statutory
obligation to report donations or gifts, this does not mean that the
statutes have conferred on directors the power to make such gifts.

Therefore, in the absence of express power it is necessary to show in some way that the gift serves the commercial purposes of the company.

(k) Exports

Where a company, or a holding company and its subsidiaries taken together, has a turnover in excess of £50,000, information as to exports must be included in the report of the directors of the company. In the case of the holding company, it is sufficient for the information to appear in the report of the directors of that company and in the report of the directors of any subsidiary which on its own exceeds a £50,000 turnover. This only applies to companies whose business consists of or includes the supply of goods; the export of goods as an agent is to be ignored. Banking and similar businesses, which do not in any way deal in goods as such, have special exemption. The information is whether or not goods have been exported by it from the United Kingdom during the year, and the aggregate values of such goods in the case of the company and of each of any subsidiaries.

(l) Directors' salaries

Companies also have to make disclosures concerning directors' pay, bonuses and benefits. The 1967 Act introduced some curious provisions (in general statistical terms) about disclosure of these. For example, details must be given of the number of directors who have no emoluments or who are paid less than £2,500, the number who receive more than £2,500 but not more than £5,000, and so on in bands of £2,500 at a time. Here again, in 1972, this rule of disclosure was revised, so that these details do not have to be given if the directors as a whole do not get a total of more than £15,000. This information has to appear in the accounts or a statement annexed to the accounts, and so is subject to the auditors' scrutiny. In addition, the chairman's remuneration must be stated.

(m) Executives' pay

Information has to be given in the same way in respect of employees earning £10,000 or more, again in bands of £2,500, excluding

directors and excluding employees who worked during the year
wholly or mainly outside the United Kingdom. The figure of £10,000
includes all earnings and the estimated money values of other benefits.

(n) Holding company

The balance sheet and accounts also have to contain a statement or
note of the name of the company which is regarded by the directors as
the ultimate holding company in their group and, if known to them,
where it is incorporated. There must also be a statement of the
identities and places of incorporation of any subsidiaries, and
particulars of shareholdings in the subsidiaries, unless the
Department of Trade will agree to non-disclosure of foreign
subsidiaries or of United Kingdom subsidiaries carrying on trade
abroad. If the directors think the particulars would be of excessive
length, they have only to include subsidiaries whose business results
principally affect the profit and loss account and assets of the group,
and to say that the list only deals with such subsidiaries. However, the
information omitted from the accounts must be added to the annual
return when it is filed at the Companies Registry. In addition the
accounts must disclose the identities and places of incorporation of
companies which are not subsidiaries but whose shares it holds, with
particulars of such shares if at the end of the financial year the holding
exceeds one-tenth in nominal value of any class of the equity share
capital. Again, there is a right to seek approval of omission of
particulars of foreign companies or United Kingdom companies
carrying on business abroad from the Department of Trade.
Similarly, if in the opinion of the directors the particulars in full would
be of excessive length, the directors need only include those whose
results principally affect the profit and loss account or assets of the
company, and must disclose that the list is so restricted. The omitted
particulars must accompany the annual return filed at the Companies
Registry.

Under the Industry Act 1975, as an alternative to outright
acquisition (which means that the Government has 100 per cent of the

profit before tax instead of the basic corporation tax which is 52 per cent at the time of writing), provision is made for manufacturing companies designated by the Secretary of State for Industry to enter into agreements for the overall conduct of their activities. To enable policy to be evolved for such agreements or for economic purposes generally the Secretary of State can serve a statutory notice requiring detailed information if he is not satisfied with the response to a request for voluntary co-operation. If a statutory notice is served copies have to go to the authorized trade union representatives as well. Information not disclosed to trade unions must not be passed on to them except for limited purposes and there are penalties for breaches of confidence, which is of particular importance since the information required includes not only current trading but forecasts. Under the Employment Protection Act 1975 the State has power to require all employers to disclose information to individual trade unions for the purpose of collective bargaining. What has to be disclosed is a matter of good industrial relations practice and ACAS (the Advisory Conciliation and Arbitration Service) has to provide guidance codes. The employer can refuse information on the grounds of security or substantial injury to the business and for certain other more intricate reasons. Prudence will dictate what can be disclosed, and where it is felt undesirable to go further, despite pressure from Government or trade unions, legal advice should be taken. Neither of these two Acts at the moment is being operated formally in view of the level of voluntary co-operation secured by the existence of the Acts on the statute book.

The essential contents of the balance sheet and profit and loss account are summarized in the Eighth Schedule to the Companies Act 1948, as amended. This is further extended, in the case of public companies quoted on a stock exchange, by the requirements of the Stock Exchange as a condition of quotations. In addition, as already mentioned, the Institute of Chartered Accountants has been attempting by a series of studies, not only to interpret, but also to extend these provisions. A useful summary, *The Financial and Accountancy Responsibilities of Directors*, is published by the General

Educational Trust of the Institute of Chartered Accountants for
England and Wales.

It should be observed that the balance-sheet does not have to follow
any particular form or lay-out, although traditionally the name implies
a statement where assets in one column are balanced against liabilities
in the other column. Modern accountancy practice tends towards
producing a series of statements. In view of the additional information
which has to be incorporated, there is increasing difficulty in
producing balance-sheets and accounts which are intelligible to the
ordinary shareholders. Far too frequently significant information is
buried in a welter of statistical information, which has also to include
in many cases the amount shown for the previous financial year.
Inevitably, shareholders tend to place reliance on informed comment,
and it is said that the Americans admire the level of informed comment
provided by the British press.

As stated, the accounts have to be the subject of a report by the
auditors. This is intended for the members at the annual general
meeting, and is read out formally before the company in general
meeting. Primarily this is a report to the meeting and not to individual
members, and the auditor must be satisfied that the directors will put
it before the members. It was customary and is now compulsory,
therefore, to include the auditors' report with the balance sheet and
accounts circulated with the notice of the meeting, which is commonly
badly attended, if the company is prospering. The auditors are under a
special duty to perform those obligations imposed upon them under
the Articles of Association, but apart from this their employment
arises from contract, which, unless it is reduced to writing, depends
on the practice of accountants as laid down by their Institute. There is
no special time-table for submission of accounts to the auditors for the
purpose of an audit. There is no duty to disclose communications
about the accounts to the shareholders, other than any notes which the
auditors may wish to put on the accounts to qualify their report. As has
already been noted, auditors are entitled to free access to all books of
account and record. Auditors are entitled to request information and
explanations from the directors and staff as may be necessary for the

performance of their duty. It is for the auditors to decide what is necessary. They can attend any general meeting of the company and speak on any part of the business which concerns them as auditors. Clearly, even in large companies, the directors must work in harmony with the auditors, and equally clearly the function of the auditors will vary enormously with the size and style of the business. Directors are entitled to take legal advice on the proposed application or working of these systems in relation to their company if they are unhappy with the approach of the auditors on any topic. Auditors are under a contractual duty of care to the company and not entitled to be arbitrary in dealing with the board.

One function of accountancy and auditing which directors may have to bear in mind for the future is management accountancy, although at present it forms no direct part of the statutory accountancy requirements. This does not relate to giving information about the results produced, but rather to the effectiveness of the utilization of the resources of the company in terms of assets and management expertise. The measurement of results in the last analysis is always in terms of profits. The point is that, with the concentration of effective control of the company in the names of the directors rather than the shareholders, there is a tendency towards complacency on the part of the board so long as profits are produced, whether or not they might be improved on. Even though the recent crude provisions of the Companies Acts have put a duty on directors to comment on important changes in value of fixed assets, shareholders who are not directly involved with the board are not usually able to make an informed judgment.

These commercial reports and accounts are not the subject of legal regulation as such, and at present are only the concern of the board, but directors who are concerned with them are under a duty to ensure that the formal statutory accounts and returns are not inconsistent with the other information available to them, and must clarify and reconcile with the auditors any differences apparent to them.

The modern tendency for most companies has been to progress from supervisory to executive boards, the theory being that the boards

of companies should consist of individuals who work in or with the
business. At the very moment when that view seemed to have
generally prevailed, it is being suggested that there is a need for
management accountancy, for directors who are not executives, and
for separate management reports to the shareholders. Directors of
public quoted companies are recommended by the Stock Exchange to
include in the reports Current Cost Accounting details, to contrast
with the information contained in the balance sheet and profit and loss
accounts prepared in accordance with the Companies Acts and taxing
statutes on a historic cost basis. As has been noted the precise methods
are still the subject of controversy. Directors should be most careful to
seek advice since it is possible, in altering accounting systems, to
attract additional taxation or fail in their duty to the shareholders.

Chapter 7

Statutory records and returns

Not only are companies under a duty, as a condition of their existence as legal persons, to keep records and to produce from these the annual accounts, but they are also subject to other obligations. These may apply to companies as such because of the peculiar nature of a company as a legal person or, although being of general application, the obligations have special features in relation to companies.

The fundamental duty of the company, as has been noted, is to deliver annual accounts to Companies House at the same time as these are laid before the shareholders for the annual general meeting, and to make an annual return to the Companies Registry once in every year and within forty-two days after the annual general meeting. It is the duty of the directors to see that these returns are filed in time, and they are liable to default proceedings if this is not done. Most small companies did not have to include their accounts with the annual return until the provisions of the 1967 Companies Act took effect, and they were in the habit of deferring approval of annual accounts from the formal annual general meeting until after taxation liabilities had been agreed. This can be a very long process, with tax laws as complex as they are. The Department of Trade were not prepared to accept this position, and as a matter of policy now insist that accounts be finalized on the basis of appropriate estimates of taxation liabilities, or with a note on the accounts where a reliable estimate cannot be made. It is up to the auditor to decide whether his report needs some qualification. If default proceedings are taken because the accounts have not been filed with the annual return, or because the annual return itself is not filed, it would be open in some cases for the directors to allege negligence on the part of their accountants, and even claim damages against them, if delays on the part of the accountants, and the Inland Revenue, were not accepted by the Department of Trade as a reason for withholding proceedings.

The form of the annual return is simply an extract of information as it appears on the statutory records maintained by the company, and does not call for any special comment as such. Where a company has numerous shareholders, it is possible to avoid listing the whole of the shareholders each year, but instead to show only changes of shareholders, and to file a complete list every third year. Where the annual report and accounts do not list all subsidiaries, this list also has to accompany the annual return.

The Department of Trade now have powers to make regulations as to the format and colour of documents for filing at the Registry and to reject documents which do not comply. Power has also been taken to accept information on microfilm, tapes or other material if the Registrar thinks fit. The Department can now by statutory instrument vary fees to be paid to the Registrar, or even prescribe fees in cases where no fees were paid before. The day may come when an impecunious litigant (or one who does not have the resources of Legal Aid available to him) may argue that the fact that information is on the register was not notice to him because he could not afford the search fees!

Corporation tax

Corporation tax, as is apparent from the name, is special to companies and is a tax on their profits. It is calculated on the profits of individual companies and is subject to allowances according to the levels of profits in fact achieved. However, with regard to subsidiary companies, so long as the holding company has not less than 90 per cent of the shares, it can take over assets from its subsidiary without paying corporation tax. If so, it takes over the asset for tax purposes on the same basis and figures as the subsidiary company held it originally; there is a statutory assumption that the transfer is at a price which represents neither a loss nor a gain. In addition, when dividends are paid by one company to another, the tax deducted is allowable as a credit in the fixing of the corporation tax which that company has to pay on its income. Where the company is a subsidiary, and the holding company has at least 75 per cent of its equity capital, there is no deduction of tax on the dividend payment to the holding company. In addition, if the holding company holds 90 per cent of its equity capital and voting shares, in fixing the corporation tax which the holding company has to pay, any income from a subsidiary which has already paid corporation tax is left out of account.

Corporation tax is really a tax both on the capital and the income of companies. Speaking generally, people pay income tax on the income received from companies, and capital gains tax on profits made when their assets are sold at more than a figure related to the original cost and later allowable expenditure, or more than a figure related to the value of the asset in April 1965 if it was acquired before that date. The rates at which capital gains tax and income tax are fixed vary, and the rules for fixing the amount of tax are different. With companies, the rules about corporation tax on income are special to companies, but the rules as to corporation tax on capital gains are basically the same as those for private individuals. This gives rise to an apparent anomaly. Basically, if a man makes a gain on the sale of an asset of £10,000 more than its value in 1965, he keeps £7,000 and pays 30 per cent in capital gains , that is, £3,000. If he earns £10,000 as a capital gain through a company which he wound up in order to obtain his money, the company pays 30 per cent in corporation tax on capital gains leaving £7,000, but he still keeps only £4,900 since he has to pay a further 30 per cent in capital gains tax on the realization of the shares by liquidation. In other words, the profit attracts an extra £2,100 in tax. These lines of distinction may be blurred by variations in taxation according to the amount of the gain and various allowances, but the fact still is that the profits in companies are taxed on a higher basis which seems irrational.

It can nevertheless be understood if it is appreciated that in 1965 the State took a partnership interest in all businesses carried on through companies, instead of merely taxing income profits. The inflation, by increasing paper values of company assets, increased the State participation in corporate businesses without compensation. On the other hand, whether or not this quasi-partnership on the part of the State is a prime cause of the inflation, the system originally instituted proved unworkable. There has been introduced complex legislation involving major grants and allowances. When these proved insufficient, because of the adverse cash flow effect, the Government introduced an allowance on a formula which excluded certain unrealized profits from taxation. The distortions produced to balance sheets and accounts prepared on historic cost figures was so great that experiments with current cost accounting have reached a stage that directors have to consider providing information on this basis as a condition of Stock Exchange quotation. In any business which involves the use or holding of capital assets that are likely to appreciate in value, the owners should discuss with their advisers most carefully how to hold such capital assets.

The forms and returns for corporation tax required by the Inland Revenue demand not only copies of the company's accounts as prepared for the shareholders, but detailed particulars on which the various tax allowances, concessions and reliefs operate. Further, when a dividend is paid to shareholders a return must be made to the Inland Revenue to account for the instalment of corporation tax which has to be paid following the payment of the dividend. This is treated as paid in advance against the corporation tax for the subsequent year of the company, and is called advance corporation tax. There used to be rules to stop the hoarding of income by companies, but now the rate of corporation tax is the same whether or not dividends are paid. Directors will have to consider what dividends the company can afford. Only in respect of non-trading income can the Inland Revenue make a claim against a company which is closely controlled. This can still be the subject of a claim for a sum equivalent to the income tax which its shareholders would have paid under an Inland Revenue formula if not enough has been paid out. If so the directors will have to explain their reasons for not paying a larger dividend, such as the money not being available at the time of the annual accounts because the company had an increased bank overdraft.

Income tax

Income tax is now as a general rule the tax payable on the income of individuals, and not companies. It is no longer the concern of companies, which previously had to deduct income tax at the standard rate from all dividends to shareholders, and account for this to the Inland Revenue. Under the advance corporation tax system, this procedure no longer applies. The shareholder has a tax credit equivalent to the advance corporation tax in respect of his dividend, which will be taken into account as an addition to his income in computing his personal tax liability which the Inland Revenue have received. Companies, like other employers, must deduct income tax from all employees' wages, including directors', and account for it on monthly returns. But there is a special rule that directors may be personally liable if the company fails to pay over to the Inland Revenue the tax deducted from wages. A director may however escape from this liability by proving it was not his responsibility to supervise the deductions, and that he knew nothing of the failure to do so.

Surtax

Surtax, or super tax, was always said to be merely a deferred
instalment of income tax, payable by those with larger incomes. It had
to be paid one year after the income tax. It gave rise to many
complications, not least of which was the problem created by the
power of the Inland Revenue to claim from a company surtax owed by
a shareholder. This was particularly important where the Inland
Revenue sought to claim that a company was hoarding income to avoid
paying dividends on which income tax would have to be paid. The
Inland Revenue had power in that case not only to collect from the
company the income tax at the standard rate, but also the surtax,
assessed at whatever rates the various individuals ought to have paid.
This could create serious problems, as the company was unable to
claim monies paid back from the shareholders. Much ingenuity went
into drafting schemes combining companies and trusts to keep down
the tax. Film stars and pop artists would enter into agreements for
companies to have the benefit of their income spread over the years
because it might for two or three years be astronomic, with tax to
match, and then non-existent as public taste changed. In addition, in
some years there was a special levy or surcharge on surtax, with the
result that some individuals found themselves with tax assessments
for more than they had earned in that year.

The passing of this tax, and its replacement with a new form of
income tax with varying standard rates, should simplify company tax
returns. Nevertheless, whenever tax represents more than, say, half
the earnings of any individual, the arrangements designed to promote
the easy running of ordinary manufacturing and trading companies
will be complicated. This arises from the natural desire of such
individuals to reduce the amount of tax that they have to pay. The laws
governing tax returns will also be many and complicated. Directors
will find that, unless one of their number is himself a specialist in
taxation and associated problems, it is essential to consult with their
solicitors and accountants on any important venture before becoming
committed. Directors who wish to reduce taxation by conducting

business from abroad, perhaps from a 'tax haven' country which gives special nil or low tax concessions, must remember that it can be an offence to expand the control of a business and should take legal advice.

At one time there was a fundamental difference between investment companies and trading companies. Only income was taxed, but while trading companies paid tax on all profits, other than on gains made by selling fixed assets of the trade such as business premises, investment companies paid no tax on gains made by selling assets, but only on the income that these assets earned. When a successful trading company was wound up, most of the income profits could be absorbed in income tax and surtax. Tax would not be paid on the gains made by selling its fixed assets or on the assets of the investment companies. Although capital gains are taxed, the taxes on income profits are assessed at very much higher rates whether the income is paid out during the life of a company or open to liquidation.

This also has a very important consequence on the sale of companies. If the shares in a trading company with large profits, not due to fixed assets, are sold for cash, the sellers should receive the price which would attract only tax on the capital gain. However, if the Inland Revenue calculate that in effect this is more than the shareholders would have received on liquidation, there was and still is power to assess the shareholders for the tax avoided by selling instead of liquidating. On any sale of the share capital of a private company for cash it was, and is therefore still, desirable to obtain clearance from the Inland Revenue, or at least to take advice on the matter. Even in the case of an investment company, it is desirable to make sure, as far as practicable, that the status of the investment company is not in doubt. With the change in 1973 to different rates for realized gains on capital as distinct from income, the treatment of values in any transaction and the allowances to be made for tax on realization of assets have increased the importance of the distinction between trading and investment companies.

Enough has been said to indicate the existence of many pitfalls for the unwary in the classification of the company, and the need for immediate advice on the form of the annual returns to be made for taxation, rather than to seek this advice at the time that a deal is about to be struck, when it may be too late to be of help.

Capital Transfer Tax

Estate duty was the tax on capital values on the death of an individual. While it was primarily the liability of his executors and of the trustees of any settlement from which he received income, it was also a liability in respect of gifts made by the dead man during his life. This has been varied and is now called Capital Transfer Tax. The tax is payable wherever capital is passed on, whether during lifetime or after death, although effectively at the lower rates it is double on death or gifts made within three years of death. The most important change is that husband and wife are treated in effect as one person. Transfers between them do not count and the tax is paid on the death of the survivor. It is no longer necessary to put shares or property in the name of a spouse to avoid death taxes. It is sufficient to leave it to the spouse either outright or to enjoy for life. On the other hand a gift of shares is treated as a gift of the difference in value of the holding of the giver before and after the gift, which is very important in the case of gifts of shares out of holdings of more than 10 per cent in private companies. These can produce tax assessments beyond the contemplation of the giver. Just as bad is the transfer of shares from one spouse to the other, which can also produce an ultimate tax disaster. Needless to say, there are ways of avoiding the new pitfalls and no such gifts should be made without legal advice. There are special rules which may enable payment to be deferred or held over, without liability to interest on the ultimate assessment because of deferment, where the gain is not realized.

Complex rules exist in respect of partial gifts, where a man retains some benefit from his gift, and in respect of gifts made within three years of death to anyone except charities. In the case of charities there is exemption for up to a substantial sum, which should be checked with legal advisers at the time, under a will, or gifts made more than twelve months prior to death, and for all gifts to charity made more than twelve months prior to death. These rules can affect companies commercially because of the amount of money that has to be raised to pay such taxes, particularly where the important asset is a shareholding in a private company which by its very nature cannot be easily sold. At this point it should be observed that the rules of valuation may seem rather harsh. Except where the shares are sold off, the Inland Revenue assesses a value by assuming an open market and a comparison with similar companies that have a stock market quotation. However, there is now an allowance in respect of controlling interests in companies owning agricultural land or manufacturing businesses, to reduce the asset value on which capital transfer tax is payable. Shares in private companies are treated in the same way as land, and duty may be paid by sixteen half-yearly instalments if the shares remain unsold.

Another problem arises in relation to cases where the shareholder has a controlling interest, or when a controlling interest passes on his death, for example, when he had given 20 per cent of the shares to his son in his life-time, and he obtains a further 40 per cent on the death of his father.

Like all things involving tax, the actual definitions of the taxing statutes are worded to catch many sorts of arrangement which seek to avoid or keep down the amount of duty payable. It is sufficient here to draw attention to these questions, and in particular to emphasize that a director holding shares in a family company should explore the possible capital transfer tax problems when making his will. It is important to emphasize the fact that he should make a will and review whether or not he should make transfers to members of his family or to trustees in his lifetime, since the way shares are left or given can affect the amount of duty to be paid. It is this which is the real problem, because a limited company cannot buy its own shares, and loans of money by a company to executors of shareholders will be treated as dividends liable to tax. The Inland Revenue do have power in the last resort in some circumstances to assess a company for the estate duty payable by a shareholder, but there is now power for the company to get the money back.

Purchase tax and VAT

Companies are also liable to pay and to make returns for various types
of excise duties. These are distinguished from income tax and
corporation tax, which are assessments on profits, since excise duties
are payable whether or not profits are made. Some arise on the import
of commodities or goods and are commonly referred to as customs
duties, being paid either on entry into this country, or upon release
from bonded warehouses where the goods are stored after import.
Others arise on manufacture, as in the case of alcoholic drinks or
petrol, unless placed in bonded store or on sale by the manufacturer.
One import duty, now phased out, was purchase tax, which was
assessed on a percentage of the price of goods supplied to retailers by
manufacturers and wholesalers. It has been retained as a special tax in
the case of cars. Generally, purchase tax has been replaced by a Value
Added Tax (VAT), which is a cascade form of tax. The idea is that
each time the goods, or components from which the goods are made,
change hands or a service is provided, tax is charged as a percentage of
the selling price. To counter unfair results, credit is allowed in respect
of the duty paid by suppliers, as shown on the invoices for the supply
of goods or services. In some cases goods do not attract VAT at all, but
it is payable on bills for professional services. There are some
transactions, such as dealings in land, which are exempt from VAT.
Other duties are those payable on tobacco, petrol and alcoholic drinks.
All these duties require the keeping of special records and returns, and
there are penalties for directors whose companies, trading in such
goods, do not observe the rules.

Although it is not the practice at the present time to do so, it might
be helpful for shareholders to be provided with copies of all revenue,
customs and excise returns made by their companies at the same time
as the annual accounts. In the case of small private companies this
usually happens, with the accountant submitting the accounts and the
tax computations in draft to the shareholders at the same time. The
chief argument against such publication to shareholders is that it
would disclose information to trade rivals, or creditors for large

companies. In these days of fuller disclosure it might be as well if shareholders could see the statements made in the name of their company; the disclosure to trade rivals and competitors could well prove a lesser evil than the present secrecy.

Other taxes paid by companies, in common with other employers, are the Social Security contributions which are payable in part by the employer and in part by the members of the staff. Here again, directors may be liable personally if returns are not made or money not paid, in the same way as they may be liable for failure to account for tax deducted from wages.

Publication by the Registrar of Companies

Publications of returns by companies to the Companies Registry now have to be included in the official *London Gazette*—in the case of Scotland the *Edinburgh Gazette*—by the Registrar of Companies, with the date of issue or receipt. These include not only the obvious documents, such as the issue of a certificate of incorporation or of registration of a legal charge, winding-up orders and the liquidator's return of the final meeting on winding-up, but also documents dealing with alterations to the Memorandum and Articles, the constitution of the board of directors and any changes, the address of the registered office from time to time, and the receipt of the annual return. Previously, it was only necessary to advertise a petition to wind up or to sanction a scheme for the company and the appointment of a liquidator in a voluntary winding-up. Apart from some 17,000 public companies, there are about 750,000 private companies in 1980 on the Register of Companies kept in Cardiff, so that the size of the *London Gazette* in the future may border upon the absurd, and the plethora of information may prove self-defeating. It may well be that this will cause grave difficulty over processing documents through the Companies Registry. The position is complicated because a company can claim that an outsider had information and was therefore bound by it. Statutory notice must be given. Furthermore, knowledge is not

presumed until the expiry of fifteen days after the official
notification—extended, if the fifteenth day is a non-business day,
such as Saturday, Sunday or a public or bank holiday, to the next
business day.

Chapter 8

Conduct at meetings

Board meetings depend for their rules first of all on the Articles. Under these it is common to find provision for a quorum, that is the number of directors who must be present in order to proceed to business, and also provision for a chairman. Everything else appears to be left to the directors, who settle their own standing orders for meetings; common law or common sense make up the rest.

Sometimes the Articles contain elaborate details for alternate directors or special voting rights. Sometimes they actually provide for formal notice of board meetings. Control of the meeting is in the hands of the chairman, not the managing director. Any director is entitled to call for a meeting of the board unless the Articles otherwise provide, and the secretary must summon a meeting if a director requires it. The board can decide to act through committees, and can ask people to attend board meetings or committees as they wish. Directors are members of the board with full rights to speak and vote, unless they have been appointed under the Articles merely as associate directors, or to some other subsidiary appointment. In such a case it is necessary to ascertain what the Articles set out as to their rights and duties.

The proper place for business is the board meeting. Only managing or executive directors, who are given power under the Articles or by the board to make decisions, can act on their own initiative. Directors are not supposed to take decisions outside the meeting, unless permitted to do so by Articles. This rule is commonly ignored in small private companies, where quite often the only formal board meeting takes place once a year to approve accounts. This is not good practice. The position is frequently dealt with by the circulating of a minute, which, after being signed by each of the directors, is inserted in the minute book. This is allowed as a substitute for a meeting, even for public companies. It is now a standard provision in Table A. It has been said that it is possible to hold a board meeting on the telephone. The answer really is that, so long as the parties agree at the time and record their decision in the minute book, the courts are unlikely to hold that the board has not made the decision. If they do not agree, then a casual meeting without notice cannot be treated as a proper meeting. Even if they do agree, but fail to make up a minute at the time, then later it may be difficult to prove it really was a proper board decision.

As far as the interests of outsiders are concerned, if they have acted in good faith, there is a rule of practice that courts will always assume in their favour that all technicalities have been duly observed. This does not prevent a director or shareholder from intervening to make a claim against directors who behaved incorrectly. If something improper has taken place, a director who was not present is not liable, and approving the minutes does not make him liable.

In a well-run company there will be regular board meetings for which notices with agendas will be sent out to directors by the secretary. Except where meetings are at regular fixed dates, all directors must be given notice at least of the fact that there is to be a meeting. If a director is absent outside the United Kingdom it is not necessary to give him notice unless he has requested that notice be given because, with modern communication, he expects to be able to be present. Under Articles in usual form it is necessary for a minimum

number of directors, a quorum, to be present throughout, and
if directors leave so that there is no quorum the board has
to adjourn.

A director must not take part in the discussion of a contract in which
he is interested, unless he has first disclosed any personal interest he
may have in it. If the director later obtains an interest, then he must
give notice at the first subsequent meeting.

Unless he is allowed to do so by the Articles, a director may not vote
on a contract in which he is interested. It may happen that there are
not enough disinterested directors to make up a quorum. In that case
the question should be referred for approval to the shareholders in
general meeting.

If the board acts on an invalid decision, an outsider who is not aware
of the invalidity is not affected save that the outsider may have a
remedy against the directors, or some of them, if the company cannot
meet its liabilities. The transaction is still valid and binding on the
company, although the directors may be liable to be sued by the
shareholders, or the company, for breach of duty. Equally, the
shareholders can approve the action by resolution in general meeting
and so ratify what the directors have done unless the transaction is
prohibited to the company by law. A subsequent board meeting with a
sufficient quorum can also do so. The attendance and decisions of the
directors, as well as any notices given to the company in relation to the
directorships, should be recorded in the minute book.

General meetings

Meetings of shareholders are usually called general meetings. The
annual meeting is the ordinary general meeting of shareholders, so any
other meeting is called an extraordinary general meeting. As a general
rule, all holders of voting shares, whatever they may be called, are

entitled to receive notice of general meetings, to attend and to vote. Their rights depend on the Articles. It is common to find that preference shareholders are entitled to notice of meetings, but generally only to attend and vote if the preference dividend is not paid or is in arrears. In addition, there is usually a right to vote on particular resolutions, if their rights or interests are affected by it.

Over the years there developed a practice of issuing shares called 'A' ordinary shares, which gave the holders all rights of an ordinary shareholder except the right to vote. Although a most useful way of enabling the dynamic personalities who were the prime movers of some enterprise to retain control whilst reducing their actual investment, it has in recent years been frowned upon as a formula by the City institutions. Quotation of further issues of 'A' shares is discouraged. For a private company or for an executive share incentive scheme, such non-voting shares or shares with restricted or suspended rights remain as a useful device. In practice with a public company it is easy, even if the 'A' shareholder is not entitled to attend and speak at general meetings, to obtain this privilege by the purchase of even one share of the voting class.

The agenda rule for a meeting is strict, in that the only business which may be dealt with by a general meeting is that of which due notice is given. Amendments to resolutions of which special notice has been given are not allowed unless due notice is given of the amendment. This means that if it is found that a special resolution as circulated is not correct the meeting may have to be adjourned to allow time for the correction to be duly notified. If, of course, all members are present, this could be waived. Control of the agenda and of the conduct of the meeting is in the hands of the chairman. Admission to the meeting, which is a private and not a public occasion, may be confined to members of the company and those persons allowed or invited to attend by the secretary on instructions of the board or by the chairman. Nevertheless, the chairman should see that a record is kept of all persons present in case of disputes as to who should vote or cast proxies. Members should be checked against a list of members. A shareholder who votes automatically cancels his proxy given before the meeting, and where shares are held jointly only one shareholder can vote. It has been known that the first named holder has signed a proxy and the second named holder has voted at the meeting, with the result that the proxy was invalidated. A representative of a company, particularly if he is a director, does not have a proxy lodged and can speak, which, unless it is specially allowed under the Articles, a proxy cannot do. But the chairman can insist on the representative, unless he is the chairman or managing director, proving his authority in the form of a certified copy of the resolution of the board of his company authorizing him to represent that company at the meeting.

The right of attendance at company meetings is a matter of interest to employees, particularly senior managers who are not directors, and trade union representatives. As the law stands, the board can keep employees out unless the company is a public company whose share can be bought on a stock exchange, in which case the purchase of one share is the price of admission. Indeed, a manager may be asked to address the meeting on some subject and then be requested to leave while his remarks are debated.

Where resolutions have been circulated for an extraordinary meeting care has to be taken in checking the votes, if a special majority is required, to see that it is validly obtained. For nearly all companies there is only one vote per shareholding in a meeting, and this is on a show of hands. It is customary for a director to call for a poll if the decision is not unanimous or nearly so. On a poll the voting is in accordance with the number of shares held, so that one man who owns 50.1 per cent of the voting shares can outvote all the rest. Any shareholder or member having 10 per cent of the voting shares (or a group together holding 10 per cent) can by law demand a poll, after the result on the show of hands, if the chairman refuses a request for a poll and does not call for one himself.

Voting has to be at the meeting and not, unless allowed by the Articles, by circulating voting papers to be deposited at the registered office. If the board has not prepared for a poll, the chairman can adjourn the meeting to enable papers to be prepared for voting at the adjourned meeting. There is no right to demand a poll on the decision of the chairman to adjourn and the chairman can order the voting papers to be sent to all members not just those present at the meeting being adjourned. His duty is to fix the place and the time, which, if allowed under the Articles, can be immediate. Members can vote even if not present when the poll was called for. The chairman will also often appoint scrutineers, who may well be members of the board, to examine and count the votes.

Private companies, particularly those that are small, so long as there is no dissension, will dispense with formal meetings. It is permissible for any company, whether public or private, to dispense with due notice of meetings if members holding 95 per cent of the voting rights at the meeting agree, except in the case of an annual general meeting when all the members holding voting rights at the meeting must agree.

Under the Articles of most private companies, resolutions can be passed simply by all the members signing a circulating minute recording that formal notice is waived and agreeing to the resolution. If there are formal meetings, then notice has to be given. Directors must be careful to see that the correct minimum notice is given.

Shareholders now have the right to complain to court if it seems that the affairs of the company are being conducted unfairly to them either alone or in common with others or that some act or omission of the company (including acts or omissions on its behalf) is or would be prejudiced. The Minister also has this power if it so appears to him or if something arises from a report made by an inspector. The court then has power to order how the company should act or conduct its affairs; this includes ordering civil proceedings by someone on behalf of the company or ordering the purchase of shares and reduction of capital.

It follows that even if a shareholder fails to carry a majority vote in meeting or to propose resolutions or amendments for a meeting, the shareholder can now apply to court for relief.

Class meetings

There is a further type of meeting, the class meeting, to take account of the rights of different classes of shareholders. It would be quite unfair to allow the ordinary shareholders to alter the rights of another class of shareholders without the consent of that class. If these rights are set out in the Memorandum of Association, they can only be altered with the consent of all the members in writing by a scheme approved by the court or as provided in the Memorandum itself. If the rights are conferred in the Articles, then it is common to find provision that the rights can be altered with the approval of a majority of three-quarters of the members of the class attending and voting at a class meeting. If the Articles are silent then it is necessary to have the consent in writing of holders of three-quarters of the class of shares or an extraordinary resolution of a class meeting. This is the same method of approval as the court would order under a scheme of reorganization. However, members who vote against, as long as they represent not less than 15 per cent of the shares of the class, may apply to the court to object. The most likely case for a minority to make such an application is when the majority of the class voting in favour also hold shares of another class which would benefit. Holders of even fewer shares could object, on the grounds that the decision was unfairly prejudicial, and could ask the court to regulate the position and perhaps order the purchase of the holding. The rules as to the conduct of class meetings, including the chairmanship, are the same as for a general meeting. Both directors and auditors are entitled to be present throughout.

Sometimes private companies have special representative director arrangements, and in such cases a representative director may be appointed or removed by a meeting of the class of shares he represents. There is no need in case of such meetings to give the special twenty-eight days' notice to remove a director. This is only required if the director is being removed under the special statutory power which exists for all companies to remove a director by simple majority of the ordinary voting members in general meetings.

Notice and quorum

For an annual general meeting, at least twenty-one clear days' notice
has to be sent through the post to all members, even dead members, at
the last registered address. Apart from this the notice depends on
business on the Agenda as follows:

NATURE OF BUSINESS	MINIMUM NOTICE
Ordinary resolution	14 days (7 days for an unlimited company)
Extraordinary resolution	14 days
Special resolution	21 days
Ordinary resolution of which special notice is also required to be given to the company (*ie* to remove directors, to appoint directors over seventy, or to elect auditors other than retiring auditor) at least 28 days before the meeting	14 days

Directors must be careful to see that the correct minimum notice is
given, and check on the meaning of 'clear days'. A director is entitled
to speak at any meeting of members. He has the special right to have a
circular sent by the company to members on notice of an ordinary
resolution to remove him from the board, but not if the removal is by
some method set out in the Articles apart from the statutory
procedure.

With all members' meetings it is necessary for a minimum number
to be present, under the provisions of the Articles. This quorum is
usually three for a public company and two for a private company
although the statutory minimum requirement, unless the Articles
provide for a quorum of one, is now two in both cases. The court, in
special cases, can order a meeting that can be validly held with one
member alone, present in person or by proxy. This means application
can be made to court, if members stay away to prevent there being a
quorum, to order a meeting. In the case of variation of class rights,
however, the minimum quorum is two members present in person or
by proxy, who must represent at least one third of the issued class of
shares; at an adjourned meeting a quorum of one is now sufficient
without application to court. However, legal advice should be taken,

as it may be that an application should be made for general remedies
on the basis of unfair conduct. Sometimes, where the Articles so
provide, different classes of shares have all to be represented in some
way. The Articles usually provide for persons present by proxy to be
counted. Normally the quorum has to be present when the meeting
starts, but the lack of a quorum caused by someone leaving does not
cause automatic adjournment, which is the usual provision for
directors' meetings. Frequently the Articles provide that if a quorum
is not present within half an hour of the time fixed for the start of the
meeting, it is adjourned by one week, or as the directors may decide,
when the numbers present shall constitute a quorum. In other cases
the meeting is dissolved.

Types of resolution

The types of resolution really depend on the Articles of Association,
but are of four kinds:

- (a) the ordinary resolution, which requires a simple majority from
  among the members present, in person or by proxy. This is
  commonly used to approve accounts, make business decisions
  and elect directors;
- (b) the extraordinary resolution. It is usually only required for the
  purpose of a class meeting to approve changes in rights or
  obligations of the members. To pass such a resolution requires a
  majority of three-quarters of the members of the class present
  who vote, in person or by proxy;
- (c) the special resolution requires the same three-quarters majority,
  but twenty-one days' notice has to be given of the intention to
  propose a resolution as a special resolution. This resolution is
  required to alter the Memorandum or Articles of Association, or
  to put a company into liquidation. With private companies,
  where formal notice can be waived, this is a convenient method
  of instantly removing a director; the resolution can include

amending the Articles for this purpose, if the Articles do not
provide for removal by special resolution; and
(d) ordinary resolution of which special notice has to be given.
These resolutions require only an ordinary majority and are
required for special purposes, that is electing a director over the
age of seventy, appointing auditors other than the existing
auditors and removing a director by ordinary resolution.

No one is entitled to be present at a class meeting apart from the
officers of the company and the shareholders of the relevant class.
Sometimes a board will agree to allow the press to be present, but even
in the case of public companies the press have no right of admission as
the meeting is classified as a private meeting. If a press representative
is present the chairman has no right to forbid reporting, but can
adjourn the meeting for the press representation to withdraw. It is
normal to arrange for stewards, if the company is not small enough for
the company secretary to deal with this himself, to check persons on
entry. Usually those attending are asked to sign an attendance list and
the members who are personally present can be identified separately
from proxies or representatives of corporate shareholders. These lists
can be important for making up information for the minutes on
attendances. In case of class meetings this can be particularly
important since, if shareholders subsequently object to court about
proposals, it is relevant to know whether those attending held shares
of more than one class. Such persons may be considered as acting
unfairly if they vote against their apparent interest in one class because
of the benefit accruing on their shares in the other class.

Minute book

The record of the conduct of meetings is kept in the minute book,
which, as has already been noted, is under the control of the chairman.
A director or member can only request that particular remarks or the
production of documents be noted in the minute book. If this is

refused by the chairman at the time, or when the minutes are read it is found that this request has been ignored, that is the end of the matter, so far as the minute book is concerned; unless the meeting is prepared to amend the record in face of refusal by the chairman. This is the case whatever may be the claims in law to be conducted over the questions. Furthermore, the minute book is only a human record, and as such it is assumed to be correct until it is proved wrong. The minute book does not of itself decide anything. It is only a record of what the chairman considers has happened at a meeting with the approval of the majority of members. Once a minute has been recorded and signed by the chairman, any subsequent correction or alteration should be made by recording a further minute, and not by changing the text. Minute books, like books of account, may be inspected by a director at any time. He can take notes or make copies for the purpose of his work or duties as director. Members can only inspect the minutes of general meetings, but they must be supplied with copies within seven days of any request. The board, when there are non-director shareholders, should keep their minutes in a separate book to those of general meetings. Care should be taken that the minute books, if they are not properly bound, are nevertheless so arranged that the insertion or removal of pages would be apparent.

At the annual general meeting, not only must the minute book be produced and the minutes of the last meeting read, but the records of directors' share dealings must be produced. A copy of each of the director's service agreements (or written memorandum setting out the terms) with the company or its subsidiaries must always be available for inspection. In the case of contracts relating to directors employed outside the United Kingdom it is sufficient to produce a memorandum giving the name of the director and the provisions as to the duration and, if the agreement is with a subsidiary, its name and place of incorporation. These are kept at the registered office, with the register of members or the principal places of business and must be open for inspection during usual business hours. In the case of public companies these copies have to be available for inspection at the annual general meeting to satisfy Stock Exchange requirements.

Where a resolution is proposed to approve a service agreement under which employment can continue for more than five years as against the company, a memorandum setting out the proposed agreement must be available for inspection at the registered office for at least fifteen days before and at the meeting. Substantial property or loan or credit transactions with directors have to be disclosed by the company's accounts, including guarantees. This also includes transactions with connected persons, who are spouses and children (including step-children) of any age. Directors are not bound, but may consider it desirable, to have the relevant documents available for inspection at the meeting. Banks which do not have to include such details in their accounts have to have such documents available for inspection at least fifteen days prior to the meeting. Records to be produced for inspection are not regarded formally as part of the minutes, but they must be available for inspection.

Alterations to the Memorandum of Association or of the Articles of Association are normally made by special resolution. If the rights of a class of shareholders are separately affected, the alteration must be approved by that class. This is done by their meeting separately to approve the alteration by extraordinary resolution, and a majority of three-quarters is necessary. As has previously been mentioned, dissenting holders with 15 per cent or more of any class can petition the court to set aside the resolution. Holders of an even smaller percentage can petition if, as far as they are concerned, the resolution is oppressive or fraudulent. A further remedy in such a case is to seek the purchase of their shares. Where the objects of the company are to be changed the court has a discretion to provide for the purchase of members' shares and the reduction of share capital or other alterations.

If an amendment to the Articles conflicts with the Memorandum it will be invalid, whether or not a court has made an order, but an action for a declaration of invalidity by the court might be sought. Nevertheless, the court is reluctant to interfere unless positive bad faith or real injustice can be proved. In order to give time for objections after the passing of a resolution, a period of twenty-one days is allowed, and there is an obligation to file a copy of the special resolution within fifteen days certified by the chairman of the meeting. In addition, the previous rule that a copy of the Memorandum of Association, reprinted in its amended form, should be filed, has now been extended by the relevant law of the European Economic Community, under which this must also be filed within the fifteen-day period. Once the Memorandum or Articles have been the subject of amendment by resolution, then a copy of the resolution must be bound up with the printed Memorandum and Articles, as amended, which a company uses for business purposes, and must be kept available for members if required. One curious provision of the new rules of the European Economic Community was that where Articles had in the past been altered and a reprinted copy not filed at the Companies Registry, then this was supposed to have been done one month after the Act came into effect on 1 January 1973. It is thought that many older, private companies may still not have complied.

Inspection by the Department of Trade

The Department of Trade, formerly the Board of Trade, have draconian powers of inspection of company records, accounts and indeed the entirety of papers and premises of a company. These powers are quite apart from, and in addition to, those conferred on the Department in the public interest, either to petition for the winding-up of a company or to bring proceedings on its behalf. The powers are informal, without the necessity of the appointment of an inspector, to enquire into some objection raised by a shareholder or other interested person. Such informal enquiries are made at the discretion of the Department, if at any time they think there is good reason so to do. This means in effect whenever the Minister thinks it socially, economically or politically expedient. No right exists to ask a court to restrain the Department, which can call for the production of books and papers specified at a time and place as set out in the notice. On the

contrary officials of the Department have a right, on arrival at
premises, to require production forthwith of any books or papers they
may call for, subject to producing evidence of their authority.
Directors must appreciate that it is an offence not to comply with such
requests.

A Department official has greater powers than the police, and can
carry out an interrogation of any officer of a company and inspect any
company books or papers at any time, without prior notice of any
intimation of proceedings against the company. Any person in
possession of books and papers (but subject to any lien) may be
required to produce them and copies may be taken. Explanations may
be required to be given by the person in whose possession they are, or
by any past or present officer or employee. If they are not produced,
the person to whom the direction was made may be asked to state to
the best of his knowledge and belief where they are. Search warrants
can also be issued to look for books and papers, and a warrant allows a
constable, together with any other person named in the warrant, to
take possession of them. Anything so taken can be held up to three
months. Any person refusing can be required to give an explanation.
It is no defence, to a prosecution for refusal to comply with a direction
or requirement, that it was unreasonable—this would only be a plea in
mitigation.

Directors who become involved in matters of this character should
take legal advice on their position in the precise circumstances. It is
important to appreciate the wide extent of the obligation to comply
with requests from the Department, as there may well be no time in
which to take advice when compliance is required at short notice.

On the other hand it must be said that the Department has used the
powers so far with caution and circumspection. In fact there has
tended to be criticism of the role played by the Department since the
introduction of these powers, because of an apparent lack of
enthusiasm to act as company Ombudsmen or Commissioners. This is
a traditional approach, and the position is confused because, if the
Department are known to be engaged on an enquiry, this is inevitably
damaging to a company's credit rating and, in the case of quoted

companies in particular, to the market price of the shares. The fact that the investigation is due to shareholders' complaints against the board may be more damaging to the position of the company than the matter of which complaint is made. The powers were really conferred on the Department because of scandals affecting the public in relation to insurance companies, and to finance companies who had dealings with them. This may explain the approach of the Department, which can rightly take the view that dissatisfied shareholders have other remedies which can be sought at their own expense, and not that of the State. Nevertheless, these powers exist. In the hands of a determined Minister, with funds to maintain the necessary staff establishment—which is one of the restrictive factors—there now exists the legal framework for rigorous State intervention in the affairs of companies generally. This should be considered in relation to the legislation for the collection of Value Added Tax, where the Inland Revenue and the Customs and Excise are now authorized to make disclosures to each other. Customs officials have authority to investigate similar to the Department's inspectors. However, neither the Inland Revenue nor the Customs and Excise may make disclosures to the Department of Trade at present.

A further turn of events has been the complaint that inspectors' reports when published, often long after investigations, may condemn an individual for his conduct, with serious economic consequences, although he has not had a trial in accordance with the principles of natural justice. In practice this criticism may have been met by the power now conferred on the Department of Trade to apply to court for a disqualification order against a person, being a director for a period not exceeding five years, for persistent default in complying with the relevant requirements of the Companies Acts. It is to be assumed that where an inspector considers that someone is unfit to be a director, proceedings will be initiated. This is in addition to the power under the Insolvency Act 1976. The requirements which are relevant are those which require any return, account or documents to be filed, delivered or sent, or any notice to be given to the Registrar of Companies. The order may be sought if a person is convicted of an offence in making returns or an order is made to make returns.

As has been noted, if the Minister considers as the result of the report of an inspector that shareholders have been unfairly prejudiced he may initiate court intervention as an alternative to seeking an order for winding up the company.

Chapter 9

The director as a representative

In theory all directors are supposed to be elected by the shareholders
to the board of the company. Sometimes particular classes, or the .
holders of particular shares or even loan stock, are entitled (either by
virtue of provisions in the articles, or by a special agreement among
the shareholders) to appoint and remove directors. Nevertheless once
so appointed directors are under a duty in law to the members
generally, but not to shareholders as individuals. Frequently directors
are first appointed to office with an existing company as a result of an
invitation from the board of directors. This is because, so long as the
maximum number of directors set out in the Articles is not exceeded,
there is a power to co-opt. In most cases, the Articles require a director
who joins the board to submit himself for election at the next annual
general meeting.

  Directors are supposed, in performing their functions, to have
regard to the interests of the company's employees in general as well as
its members. This is defined, however, as a duty to the company alone

and enforceable in the same way as any other fiduciary duty owed to
the company by its directors. Directors have always had such a duty, if
by having regard to employees' interests—for example, by setting up
an employees' share scheme—the company's interests are advanced.
There was a problem if a company was going to cease to trade, since
paying monies, beyond statutory obligations, could not be said to be in
the company's interests. As the law now stands, unless the power to
make such payments is expressly given to the directors under the
Memorandum or Articles of Association, this is a matter for decision
by the members. Generally, the change in the law removed technical
restrictions on the directors, in dealing with employees, acting in
accordance with good commercial practice. The duty so to act is owed
to the company by the board so that employees have not been given
any new right, as such, for which they can sue.

Once on the board a director is, in some senses, a trustee for the
shareholders, even if he is not a shareholder. If he does acquire shares,
the director is not supposed to use his special position to gain
advantage over other shareholders. A director, whether or not he has
shares in the company, may be employed by the company in its
business as distinct from simply being paid fees for his services as a
director. There are therefore different types of directors such as:

(a) directors with substantial shareholdings directly interested in
    the conduct of the business;
(b) directors who have been elected to watch the interests of
    shareholders, who have at least the minimum share qualification,
    but who receive little more than out of pocket expenses;
(c) directors (who may or may not have had to take up a share
    qualification) elected by the shareholders and receiving
    substantial fees to supervise the activities of management and
    staff;
(d) directors (who may or may not have had to take up a share
    qualification) appointed by the board to be part of executive
    management and paid accordingly as employees with contracts
    as such; and

(e) directors appointed to represent special interests, whether a special class of shareholders, loan or debenture holders, or even some outside interest such as a supplier or important customer or a government department or statutory board.

It is essential to appreciate that since there is no system for strict classification of directors, it is difficult to allocate individuals to a particular class. In fact the different types may be found (with variations) on the boards of both public and private companies.

The total voting power as shareholders which a board of directors in fact owns and controls is a critical factor in the conduct of business. It is self-evident that if an individual or a few close members of a family or a partnership have an effective voting block, then the board is really in charge of the situation. For this purpose an effective block in practice is usually regarded as about 35 per cent or more. It may happen that one individual, perhaps with his family trust, will have a block of this order and others on the board may bring the board total to more than 51 per cent, but in practice it is likely that the holder of a 35 per cent block will have effective command, subject always to conflicting personalities. In all such cases the interests of the rest of the shareholders should be safeguarded, because of common interest, unless the holder of the key block draws his livelihood from the company as remuneration for services. In cases where the board members do not own or control such a block of shares, directors may nevertheless have an identity of interest with the shareholders because, particularly in the case of the larger and more successful companies, their personal capital fortunes are bound up with the success or failure of the company. To a considerable extent this healthy factor has been eroded by taxation policy in the past which has sought to distinguish between dividends (unearned—'bad') and salary (earned—'good'). This led to many business distortions, not least of which was the large shareholder/director waiving dividends, because the cash would be wholly absorbed by taxation and not be available as savings for re-investment if taken direct.

It follows that in most cases now it is common to find individual directors who hold few, if any, shares in the company, perhaps a minimum share qualification where this provision has been retained in the Articles. Further, frequently in the case of the companies which command the economic heights of the economy, the entire board has a very few per cent of the company's shares. Some attempts to remedy this situation, by introduction of staff share incentive schemes by which the cost of acquiring shares is reduced, have been made, but again the vagaries of taxation fashion have undermined the effectiveness of this as a means of ensuring the directors identify their economic interests with the shareholders they are supposed to represent.

At least in theory a director appointed to the board of a company in which the board has effective control should be working for the shareholders and representing their interests. In the cases, which seem to be the majority, where this is not so, the directors form, or are a part of, management who are executive employees. Under the definition of directors' duties, which clearly now include the interests of the company's employees in general, the directors are entitled to consider themselves in conjunction with but not as separate from other employees. Such boards are self-perpetuating and run on the basis of satisfying the shareholders, and in practice do not consider their interests in priority to management. However, such boards live dangerously, in particular when take-over bids are made, and they then have to justify their position to the shareholders. It is in these cases that a bid suddenly galvanizes the board into making dazzling disclosures of company prospects. It is also in these cases that directors may seek to secure service agreements, which will enable them to collect the maximum compensation for the loss of office, likely to follow upon the rationalization that is usually the commercial justification for the bid. Under the codes dealing with take-over and other similar mergers the board are entitled, at the expense of the company, to engage specialist advisers to fend off and advocate opposition to bids. The scope for such action is limited now that agreements for a duration of more than five years against the company have to be approved by shareholders in general meeting. Conversely if a company is taken over whose directors already have long-term service contracts, the validity of the contract remains unaffected and does not have to be re-approved by the shareholders of the acquiring company.

In legal terms all directors may appear to hold the same position, but the difference on analysis should be clear. Some boards of directors represent the shareholders and supervise the management, which is conducted in the main by non-board executives, although management may be represented by an employed managing director and perhaps a finance director. Some boards are deeply engaged in management with only one or two non-executive directors who act in a supervising or consultant capacity, frequently the case where one or two individuals have an effective voting block. Many boards consist exclusively of management, and when they come to the shareholders' meeting they represent the executive management reporting to shareholders. The real problem is often that shareholders are too fragmented to take an effective dissenting view (except in case of obvious disaster), unable to supervise what is happening, and heavily dependent on the auditors to alert them to disaster.

In all these situations the director relies heavily on a few key provisions of the Articles, which must always be borne in mind. The first is whether or not the Articles allow his fellow directors to vote him off the board. A fairly common provision is that a director is deemed to vacate office if the rest of the board vote for his resignation. Such a provision means that where the board does not have effective voting control, nevertheless a dissenting director can be removed without publicity or reference to the shareholders. This is most convenient from the point of view of a directors' oligarchy. A director so removed cannot have the shareholders circularized at the company's expense, which is the case if the clause does not appear in the Articles, and the board have to win a vote to remove their critic. The second provision is the general prohibition against taking part at a board meeting in business in which the director has in any way, whether directly or indirectly, an interest in a contract or a proposed contract. The new rules about types of contract which are prohibited or which require special approval by shareholders have to be kept in mind. A director should therefore disclose not only his interest but also that of a company with which he is associated, his spouse or children (including illegitimate or step-children) under eighteen (as well as the partners of any such person) or a trusteeship where the trust could benefit any such person. Curiously, the statutes do not extend this to parents or siblings, but if relatives are likely to reward or show favour a director should disclose this as well. The type of company which is associated for this purpose is one in which the director and persons connected with him have one fifth of the share capital or voting power. The actual interpretation of the wordings and application to particular circumstances is complicated and if in doubt a director should take legal advice. A director must declare his interest at the first meeting it is under consideration—although he can give a general notice that he is a member of a specified company or firm. This will suffice for all future contracts with it. In addition, unless the articles specially provide otherwise, an interested director is not to be counted for the purpose of constituting a quorum for the meeting, nor is he allowed to vote, except on provisions to indemnify him for actions on behalf of the company or where his interest in the other company is merely as a holder of office or of shares. The company in general meeting can waive prohibitions. There is a special prohibition about acquisitions to or disposals by directors or persons connected with him of non-cash assets worth more than 10 per cent of the net assets (if that exceeds £1,000) or exceeds £50,000 without the initial approval of the shareholders in general meeting. It follows that in the ordinary way a director ought not to take part in board decisions in which he has an interest. This has to be relaxed if the director is to act as an effective representative of an interest. In some companies the position is reflected by a holding company/operating subsidiary system, and in others by a single board with management functioning as a series of sub-committees which conform to the division of activities of the undertaking as a whole. Some British companies, particularly those with American holding companies, now have Audit Committees. The Accountants International Study Group on current practice in the

United States, Canada and the United Kingdom considered that the advantages of a liaison committee between non-executive directors and the auditors outweigh the disadvantages. The important point is that it is a requirement of the New York Stock Exchange, and is a method of overcoming what was a criticism made on investigation of British companies, namely the paucity of communication between the auditors and the directors. Auditors deal with the managing director or general manager, and except where there is a management account system they have no regular means of referring to the board problems or differences with management. Boards, despite the antipathy this may arouse on the part of executive management, should consider whether one or more of the non-executive directors, as a sub-committee, should not supervise accounting and auditing procedures, and review accounts before their presentation to the main board. In the case of public companies it should increase confidence to know that directors of reputation, whose presence on the board is part of its image for credibility, were involved in this function. It has been demonstrated in the past, in the absence of machinery of this kind, that such directors are otherwise helpless to restrain ruthless colleagues because the information which might entitle them to act cannot reach them. On the other hand, in the case of large, conglomerate groups, major industrial or commercial companies, it is difficult to see how such work can be undertaken effectively by non-executive directors. If they are voted large fees they are effectively executive directors because so much of their time has to be directed to this work. It may be that the recognition of professional status for secretaries of public companies will result in them assuming more of a supervisory and liaison role between the board—as distinct from the executives—and the auditors.

In West Germany arrangements are formalized by a two-tier board system which has aroused much interest. The German stock corporation, *Aktiengesellschaft*, which is styled *AG*, is based on a law established under the Nazi regime. It provided, in accordance with the National Socialist doctrine, the right for workers to be involved in the companies in which they work, and was rewritten in 1948. The *AG* is now directed and represented by a board of management, which can be a single person (who thus approximates to a managing director reporting to a non-executive board) or two or more directors (one of whom acts as chairman) who have to take decisions on internal management by majority decision. The board of management is appointed, supervised and removed by a second board which does not perform a management function. It does have power to require that its approval be obtained to certain types of transaction. There is a distinct cleavage between the two boards because no one may be a member of both and indeed members of the supervisory board may not serve in an executive capacity of the *AG*.

The membership of the supervisory board is three or a multiple of three up to twenty-one, which is the maximum allowed in the case of an *AG* with a capital of twenty million or more deutschmarks. The members of the supervisory board are elected or appointed by the shareholders by majority vote except for the labour representation which is required for *AG*s with 500 or more employees. It is a custom for the supervisory board to include outsiders such as a bank official, but no one may be a member of more than ten such boards. There are further restrictions; for example, the legal representative of a subsidiary may not be a member of the supervisory board. The labour representatives are elected by the employees and have the same rights and duties. There is no right to be on committees of the supervisory board although two members always have the right to call for board meetings and to force the board of management to give specific information.

The auditors examine the books each year and report to the management board. In the course of their audit they have to report on facts which endanger the existence of the enterprise and, subject to comment on the report, the auditors attest it. The examination report, the report of management and the financial statements are next submitted by the management board to the supervisory board, together with the proposed appropriation of retained earnings which is to be presented to the shareholders. The supervisory board in turn considers these and may request the auditors to participate. The supervisory board then reports within one month for the shareholders' meeting, giving its opinion on results and its approval or non-approval of the financial statements. It is the responsibility of the board of management of the *AG* to call the annual meeting to receive the financial statement. The auditors must participate in the proceedings of determining the annual financial statements at the shareholders' meeting. They are not obliged to give information to a shareholder, although they have to attest the statements. If they refuse, notice of this fact must be given to the shareholders. It will be observed that on this system the employees have no powers of determination.

The German structure should be compared with the controversy aroused by the Bullock Report on Industrial Democracy which proposed labour representation on British boards. Many people have criticized this report, saying that it suffered from a doctrinaire approach to this complex subject because of its terms of reference. This called for consideration of how labour should be represented, but did not provide for a study of the structure and organization of boards of directors in commerce and industry with a view to reform or reorganization. The German model, which would allow for labour integration with management, originally was favoured in discussions on EEC Draft Directives for harmonizing Company Law. It had also been claimed that there was considerable confusion of thinking as to whether the labour representatives should themselves have to be employees of long standing or whether they could be outside specialists chosen by the staff. One of the most important issues raised by the Bullock Report, and never considered, was the extent to which the board of directors represent management as an end in itself, with its career hierarchy, and not the shareholders' interests at all. It may well be that if labour is to be represented, the shareholders too should have a right to representative directors, for whom employment by the company would be a disqualification. It will be appreciated that the Bullock Report (which contained proposals for a single board system with direct equal representation of employees and shareholders who would then nominate some independents, the so-called 2X + Y formula) bore no relationship in practice to the *AG* nor indeed to British company experience to date.

It has been observed that those companies which would like to follow the German model in the interest of good labour relations, can, under the Companies Acts, adopt articles on the lines of the *AG* without the need for any further legislation on the subject. The chief difficulty which most companies face, however, is the fragmented character of the British trade union movement, which is organized for historic reasons on a trade or craft basis rather than on a plant or company basis with consequent antagonism in demarcation disputes and restrictive practices. The view has been expressed by some that, for a modern representation system to function effectively, it would seem desirable for there to be a matching reorganisation of the trade union movement itself. It may also be true that the difference between German and British models is more one of semantics than is appreciated where companies consist of a board in which the directors in the main represent the shareholders and management is conducted by a general manager who may be called a managing director, supported by commercial finance and personnel executives who control the divisions of the business through sub-committees. Such a board would find the top management in fact not only running the business, but representing the interests of the staff. It is essential to appreciate that whatever may be the views of British commerce and industry, dynamic changes are in train because of the drive towards European harmonization. Boards which are trying to anticipate these developments should scrutinize the representative status of their directors and consider how far, by judicious use of the committee system, they can anticipate and derive benefit from the German model. The minimum necessary change, which may have to be considered as the EEC directives are developed to produce conformity with the laws relating to limited companies, is to establish a council to represent employees in discussions with the board. It should be noted that as Community studies have progressed there has been a change in approach and the advantages of a unitary board system reappraised. This may well mean that the risk of a directive compelling a two tier system has now receded.

Chapter 10

Public companies

The essential difference between public and private companies lies in the principle governing their ownership. With a public company there is generally no restriction on who may own its shares. Anyone willing to pay the price to the seller may purchase. With a private company, usually only someone approved by the board, or complying with special requirements in the Articles, or both, is allowed to purchase. Because public company shares are a market place commodity, susceptible of being used in so many different ways to deceive a purchaser, special rules are compiled to protect dealers in and purchasers of such shares. Some rules are propounded by the State as laws, some by the market place, some by the professional dealers. The object is to provide for orderly marketing, and to improve confidence in the honesty and integrity of those concerned in the operations. A public company now has to have limited liability and share capital of which the authorized minimum is at least £50,000. If, as a result of a reduction in share capital it has less, then a public company has to wind up or re-register as a private company. Public companies may indeed also own or control much of their business through subsidiary private companies. Although this can be a confusing factor, such subsidiary companies are grouped for accounting purposes with the public company. It is undoubtedly a feature of public companies that the basic unit in which dealing takes place is usually a minute fraction of the issued share capital and is easy to buy or sell on the basis of published information.

With the private company, very different considerations apply. Anyone investing in a private company, unless he is already closely associated and familiar with it, should only do so after investigation by professional advisers. Usually what will be involved is a significant proportion of the whole company which, by its very nature, is not easily saleable. This is what makes investigation so important, as much of the information which is highly relevant for such a transaction is not readily available. The private company was introduced in 1908 primarily to allow small businesses the privilege of limited liability coupled with perpetual succession, so that the business does not die with the parties, and to enable ownership to be divorced from management. There is much overlap between public companies and private companies, which are for the most part governed by the same laws. However, the vast majority of private companies (excluding those owned by public companies) because of the smaller scale of their business, commonly function on different lines and do not have the same sort of long term dividend record. On the other hand some private companies may utilize resources larger than many public companies.

So far as directors are concerned, the important difference comes in relation to the obligations requiring provision of information to the stock exchanges. This applies in the first instance on the commencement of business. Directors of public companies have to warrant the correctness of the prospectus, and to see that all the additional information required in excess of the statutory provisions is duly provided. This is a condition to be met in order that members may have the right for their shares to be dealt on a stock exchange. The Stock Exchange may refuse to permit dealings if its requirements are not met in the first instance, or may suspend dealings if at any time there is non-compliance.

Apart from the direct prohibition against shares being offered for sale to the public, transfers are usually restricted to persons approved by the board, or to special groups under the Articles. There was also a rule that the total number of members was not to exceed fifty, excluding employees and former employees, but that is no longer operative. Two or more persons holding shares jointly count as one. Because of this control on transfers and on numbers, private companies could not issue bearer shares in the past. There are added differences, as public companies have to maintain a special register of persons having 10 per cent or more of the shares of any class, and the terms of employment of directors are available to the public by the purchase of a nominal shareholding. Anyone can exercise the right of a shareholder to inspect directors' service contracts, or the memorandum setting out the terms of their employment if there are no contracts, but in the case of private companies it is necessary first to purchase a share, which may not be easy. Indeed because of this sort of problem it is unlikely that many private companies will relax the directors' control of transfers.

The position of public companies, from the point of view of the director who has no significant shareholding, is peculiar. In many companies all the directors between them may have only 5 to 10 per cent of the shares. In practice, the directors control the company and can handle its affairs to an extent which is quite beyond a director of a private company who has a similarly small holding. In the vast majority of cases, the latter is an employee with readily identifiable proprietors in the business, who probably know each other and may well be related. Much has been written on the subject of the managerial revolution and on the development of financial responsibility inherent in these circumstances.

It was the practice with public companies to appoint men of known standing and responsibility to ensure that the public was represented on the board by disinterested directors. However, this practice has been discouraged by the popular press, who have criticized those appointed to the board of directors who do nothing but attend board meetings. Ironically, this led to an abortive private member's Companies Bill in the House of Commons in 1972, which would have provided that large companies should have at least two or three directors who had no executive capacity and who would report separately to the members. Directors must remember that whilst a private company may trade from the date of incorporation, public companies may not start business or borrow until after the issue of a certificate of satisfaction which complies with the statutory rules as to the provision of sufficient capital to enable it to carry on business. The Companies Registry used to have particulars of a company with a share capital of one penny, divided into two shares of one halfpenny each which, since it was private, was incorporated with that as capital. Needless to say, most public companies form and use private companies as subsidiaries because of these provisions. A public company used to require not less than seven members, but now requires only the same as a private company which needs at least two; and the penalty of having less than the minimum number is that, after six months, limited liability is lost until the minimum is restored. Strangely enough, a company incorporated without limited liability is subject to the same rule, and must have two members on incorporation—although of course it does not matter if afterwards the membership is reduced to one. Provided that he has a company secretary, it is possible for Joe Biggs to incorporate an unlimited company in the name of Joe Biggs, and become the sole director and shareholder. He is then effectively at the same time two people with the same name! Following the changes in company law due to the European Economic Community rules, when he writes as a company he must use stationery which not only gives his name and address but also the company's registered number and where he is incorporated.

At this point it should be noted that there is liberty to convert, subject to statutory procedures, from a private company to a public company or vice versa. While a company can change from public to private and back again as often as it likes, the change from limited to unlimited can only take place once. If a company is registered as unlimited it may, subject to power being provided in the Memorandum of Association, buy and sell its own shares. In certain circumstances re-registration as an unlimited company may be a way for directors to return capital to shareholders without the expense of an application to court on a scheme of arrangement. It is modern practice, because of convenience, to form companies as private companies and to convert to public companies later.

Directors of private companies do have much greater control of the membership of the company in one sense, in that usually under the Articles of Association they have the power to decline to accept a transfer of shares to a new member of the company. This does not apply to public companies, whose boards, in order to secure a quotation on the Stock Exchange, must accept as members whoever is named in the transfer. There were a few exceptions to this, now generally disappearing. One was the Solicitors' Law Stationery Society Limited whose membership was confined to practising solicitors. This restriction was abolished and, as was to be anticipated, the company was promptly taken over on a bid!

The Stock Exchange—Share and Loan Department

Quoted companies are subject to special rules if their shares are to be dealt in upon a recognized stock exchange. The Stock Exchange, London, achieves this by means of the listing agreement, which incorporates the standard set of conditions in the arrangements for quotation of the securities of the company, varied from time to time as circumstances require. The procedures on such subjects are followed substantially by the Scottish Stock Exchange and the provincial exchanges, and lay down a series of requirements before quotation is permitted. Not the least of these are that the companies be of an appropriate size, have established profits and produce biographical details of themselves and of their directors. Once a company's shares are quoted, the board must follow the required pattern of provision and release of information, not only as to the issue of new shares, but also as to important dealings with their business and the size of their profits. In addition the Share and Loan Department of the Stock Exchange expect the Articles of Association to carry a number of provisions restricting and defining the powers of directors, particularly as to borrowing limits, which must not be exceeded without the approval of the shareholders in general meeting. A company whose Articles require amendment to conform with changes in stock exchange rules is sometimes allowed to carry on with business in hand, possibly with a bonus issue, if the board gives an undertaking not in fact to use the wider powers permitted under its existing Articles pending the formal amendment of them. Following this through recent years, the Share and Loan Department are reluctant to advise the Council of the Stock Exchange to permit dealings in ordinary shares which do not carry voting rights. The result of this has been that except in cases where public companies already have such shares in issue and which are quoted, and are merely issuing bonus shares, it is not really possible to secure a quotation.

The approach to the Share and Loan Department is normally through a stockbroker. This system is not of itself capable of coping with market operations by skilled or devious operators or of policing the machinations of the unscrupulous. The Department of Trade have wide powers of investigation and there are penalties laid down in criminal law for circulars distributed by unauthorized dealers and even for inaccurate statements, but these may only operate after the event.

With the increasing liaison between the accountants' Institutes and the Share and Loan Department, new disclosure requirements have been developed for public quoted companies, with which boards are pressed to comply although these are not statutory or common law obligations. Professional advice should be taken in all circumstances where the board are concerned about adverse effects of public disclosure, as informal waivers may be negotiated.

It is also possible for shares in public companies—and even some private companies—to be bought and sold through a stockbroker under special rules which allow members of the Stock Exchange to transact specific bargains in unlisted stocks on the basis that buyer and seller did this at their own risk. The essential difference for this type of transaction is that the deals are negotiated and not based on a listed or quoted price and jobbers do not have to be involved, although, in more active shares or where there is a large holding to be sold off in small amounts they may do so. This unlisted securities market is of growing importance. It is of course expensive to acquire a quotation and a company has to take an active part in practice in maintaining an informal and satisfactory market, which may not be appropriate for companies. By this method investors do have access to a wider market even though the company itself is not involved. Another development has been the publication by the Stock Exchange of the Official List of bargains struck under this system and a special notice board in the Stock Exchange reveals in whose shares there has been a dealing, and the sponsoring broker or a recognized agent. Shares in companies whose quotations have been suspended can also be bought and sold under this system after the lapse of some months. This has been developed so that the Stock Market provides a new market for unlisted companies who comply with regulations and criteria published by the Stock Exchange. This is called the Unlisted Securities Market for companies who comply with regulations about entry to the market and flow of information and behaviour thereafter. Basically such companies are expected to have at least 15 per cent of their shares out with the public and to have traded successfully for two or three years. The system for dealing in shares of other companies continues as at present. This initiative by the Stock Exchange is wholly compatible with the new form of public company which does not have to produce a prospectus or statement in lieu of prospectus. It is also a response to the activities of certain authorized dealers in securities who have been making a market primarily for investors to buy and sell shares in substantial, successful companies before such companies have obtained a quotation, although other purposes are also served.

The Take-over Panel

In the United States of America there is a very different system, with a state-sponsored Securities Exchange Commission which exists to investigate suspicious activities and to verify all published statements, as well as a system of law which puts a premium on civil enforcement by lawyers. This makes it practical to sue on behalf of 'a hundred thousand suckers each of whom has been clipped for a dollar'. In any reference to the United States system it must also be appreciated that public limited companies can trade in their own shares. In the United Kingdom this is absolutely prohibited although this could change. In England, the solution is, as usual, a committee system. Established by the Stock Exchange in consultation with the Governor of the Bank of England and the Issuing Houses Association (a mixture of all those city institutions concerned with the sale of shares on the Stock Exchange), this committee is called the Take-over Panel. It was created in 1968, after adverse comment as to the way in which target companies when faced with a bid were issuing shares to third parties, or a competing bidder or large shareholder would buy or deal in shares of the target company so as to shut out the other bidder for control. This created chaos in share quotations and disturbed orderly marketing, the result being that shareholders belonging to some groups might secure advantageous treatment.

The Panel has no power, other than to scold or perhaps exert influence on an informal club basis, although the Issuing Houses Association and some other city groups have indicated that they may suspend an offending member. This means that if a city dealer infringes the code he is likely to find all sorts of minor difficulties in doing business in the future. The smaller dealing organizations are thus more likely to be deterred than the larger and more influential. It also means that the innocent clients of that city dealer may, in other ordinary business, be placed at a disadvantage or caused more expense in practice, unless they take their patronage elsewhere. Whilst the Take-over Panel system is supposed to avoid the problems of legal regulations, it does also seem to be a system which, by its very nature, is paternalistic and not given to equality of treatment. The Stock Exchange may suspend dealings on its recommendation, but this is of limited value, since suspension of dealing may well harm the small shareholders whom it is attempting to protect.

Nevertheless the Panel has succeeded in working out codes of practice which are honoured more in the observance than the breach. The merchant banks and large investors find it convenient to comply, and fear the introduction of a Securities Exchange Commission which would be likely to be inhibiting and costly, because of the practices which would have to be followed. Instead, there is a general reliance on honesty and integrity which is so much a feature of the dealings in the City of London. It is also true that the original Take-over Code was said by the Director-General of the Panel at the time not to be a legal document, but was intended instead to be honoured in spirit. Lawyers were warned off. However this spirit proved a will-o'-the-wisp, and the code has been frequently rewritten in less ambiguous terms, in the light of experience.

In bid situations, circulars to shareholders and statements are the subject of definite criteria. Directors involved in such matters should seek advice, not merely from their financial advisers but also separate independent legal advisers, as to their responsibilities and duties to their shareholders. It can well happen that what is counselled in the interests of the market may well run counter to the interests of the shareholders and the employees. The market may well want to see the highest bidder win and the rules are so devised, but the board, for example, may well want to protect employees against redundancy, preserve a family association or simply not wish to be absorbed by a foreign or multinational corporate group. Directors should be extremely cautious about accepting legal advice as part of a package from a merchant bank. However skilled and specialized this advice may be, it should be considered in addition to, and not in substitution for, the advice of the professional advisers who deal with the business affairs of the company in normal circumstances.

Prospectus and statements in lieu

Directors may also send circulars to the members and families of a company, its employees and families or its creditors; but if the circular is to go to anyone else it must either be approved by the Department of Trade—to whom it can be submitted by the company, its solicitors, or accountants—or be sent through the agency of an authorized dealer, which includes stockbrokers, banks and others licensed by the Department. These provisions were intended to ensure that offers for shares or securities were made only by a prospectus in appropriate form. Public companies, who alone may offer shares for sale or subscription to the general public, must in practice comply with these rules, which are extended beyond the statutory requirements by conditions imposed by the Share and Loan Department of the Stock Exchange as a condition of quotation. A public company which does not require a quotation can avoid this extension. Sometimes companies, particularly companies being groomed for a successful placing on the Stock Exchange, used to file a statement in lieu of prospectus at the Companies Registry in order to comply with the statutory conditions. With the new procedures it is only necessary to obtain a certificate of satisfaction of capital requirements. Publication with a prospectus by advertisement can come at a later stage. Indeed some such companies have been known to produce a full prospectus and to have substantial dealings conducted by some authorized dealer before the shares are brought to the market. It has been argued that this assists some companies to raise risk capital where the expense of a full Stock Exchange launch is not justified.

Advertisement procedure may be in one of three forms which may be varied to meet the circumstances:

(a) an 'offer for sale', where the public generally are invited to fill in and submit applications for shares;

(b) a 'placing', where the public generally are not invited to buy shares, although considerable numbers of shares are being sold through stockbrokers and others to their clients; and

(c) an 'introduction', where the shares are already widely held and the object is merely to provide the public with the information to enable dealings to take place. This latter operation, so far as directors are concerned, is merely a matter of timing.

It will be observed that directors of unquoted companies may need to consider whether to arrange a placing of shares with an authorized dealer or in the Unlisted Securities Market; legal advice as to the implications should be sought. Security marketing (for it can hardly be described as an industry) is developing a system of law over and beyond the internal rules of the recognised stock exchanges, not least because the big investment institutions have formalized their own arrangements to buy and sell direct. This subjects company officials to more legal restraints and implications in that they must be alert to situations which may arise and which may require specific legal advice to be taken by the board.

Chapter 11

Winding-up, insolvency and bankruptcy

A company can be killed off by one of three means: striking-off the register of companies, dissolution on a scheme without winding-up, or winding-up.

The main difference is that striking-off is basically a penal procedure, under which the assets vest in the Crown, which may or may not disclaim them. This usually occurs in consequence of failure to file returns, although the court also has power to order striking-off. It is, however, sometimes used to get rid of dormant companies with no assets or liabilities, rather than incur the expense of winding-up. The Registrar, if asked, will adopt the procedure subject to assurances about the state of affairs. Once a company has been struck off, it is necessary for a director or shareholder to apply to a court for restoration to the register. The decision is in the discretion of the court. They may seek to see that various penalties are enforced as well as payment of the expense of the court application, where the striking-off has for instance taken place because of failure to file an annual return.

Dissolution is also possible as part of a scheme of arrangement involving a group of companies. There is a power which allows the court to order the dissolution of a company, without winding-up, because the assets of the company and responsibility for its liabilities have been transferred to another company.

Winding-up can arise in three different ways:

(a) as a result of a decision by the shareholders to wind up, either because the company is to be discontinued and the net assets, after paying creditors, distributed to its shareholders, or because the company cannot meet its commitments and this is admitted;

(b) because creditors petition the court to wind up the company on the grounds of insolvency; and

(c) because the court orders winding-up at the request of the company, or as a result of complaints from shareholders or the Department of Trade on the grounds of public interest or by reason of shareholders' disputes, or where the court thinks this is the just and equitable solution, or at the request of the Official Receiver.

Voluntary winding-up

The first method is described as voluntary liquidation, whilst winding-up by the court is compulsory liquidation. Where the liquidation is voluntary, the shareholders appoint the liquidator at their meeting, when the decision to liquidate to be effective must be passed as a special resolution. Before this is possible a majority of the directors must make a formal declaration of solvency which has first to be filed with the Companies Registry. This declaration has to include a statement of the assets and liabilities, and the directors must confirm that they have investigated the affairs of the company and that it will be able to pay its debts within twelve months.

In all cases a liquidator is appointed, but where the liquidation is voluntary, the liquidator is nominated in the first instance by the shareholders. If the company is solvent the liquidator is usually named in the resolution to enter into liquidation. If the company is insolvent, the liquidator is elected by the first meeting of creditors, which in that case should be convened by the secretary at the direction of the board.

A company is insolvent, as a matter of legal definition, if it is unable to pay its debts when the same fall due for payment. Very many companies, because of the state of their assets, would be unable to pay their debts, if demanded. This is not necessarily insolvency. Directors are liable to conviction for a criminal offence if they continue the trading of a company knowing it to be insolvent. If in doubt, their duty is to consult the auditors, and directors must be seen to act with reasonable prudence. In particular, directors should not allow the company to take new credit until the accounting advice has been obtained. Furthermore, if it is found that the company carried on business with intent to defraud creditors, or for any fraudulent purpose, any director or any other person who was knowingly a party is personally responsible for all or any of the debts. On the other hand recklessness alone will not make a director liable to a creditor although he might be sued by shareholders.

Once a liquidator is appointed, the directors and secretary cease to have any power or authority over the affairs of the company. Even the sealing of deeds is witnessed by the liquidator. However, directors may be called upon to prepare accounts and to give explanations of their conduct.

Winding-up under supervision of the court

It is possible that creditors or shareholders will not be satisfied to proceed by way of purely voluntary liquidation. In this case it is possible for them to petition for the company to be wound up compulsorily when, following a court order, the Official Receiver will take over the conduct of the liquidation. The court may, if the judge thinks it appropriate, merely make a supervision order. In fact it is possible to apply for a supervision order direct, and this is sometimes done as an alternative, or in opposition to, an application for compulsory winding-up by the court. It may be sought because there are allegations of bad faith, or simply because it is desired to have a second liquidator because of dissatisfaction with the acting liquidator. On such an order all court actions are stayed, and the judge usually orders progress reports and requires that all professional fees be approved by the Court Registrar.

On a creditor's petition to the court, the directors have the power to instruct lawyers to appear on behalf of the company to contest the application. The directors may even cause the company to appeal against an order for it to go into compulsory liquidation. The creditor has to prove his case, and can succeed by proving his debt and showing that it has not been paid after proper demand has been made.

Similarly the other petitions to the court must show good cause for the order. In the case of a shareholder the court can make an order if it is thought just and equitable. As the law now is, if director-shareholders have been conducting the affairs of a private company as if they were in partnership and then quarrel, a judge can order the company to be wound up on a petition by one or other of the partners. If the shareholder has been unfairly treated, the judge, if formally requested, can order that one side buy out the other at a price to be worked out as he thinks best. Further, the court has power, if money or assets have been misapplied by the directors or other officers, or the directors have been negligent or behaved wrongfully, to order them to account with interest or pay compensation. This could include a claim against an auditor who misled the directors.

The liquidator and receivers

Upon a petition to the court, a liquidator will be appointed. This will frequently be the Official Receiver, at least until the petitioners agree upon some other person who can be substituted by a court order.

The duty of the liquidator is to gather all the assets and then deal with the liabilities in accordance with the statutory priorities. At the end of this process the liquidator has to render a final account, upon the filing of which the company will be wound up and struck off the register. At the same time, in addition to making a report summarizing the company's affairs and commenting on the history, the Official Receiver may report that he considers offences have been committed by directors or others involved. The court can subsequently order the directors to attend court and be examined publicly on oath. Normally a person is not called unless the Official Receiver considers he has been involved in fraud and shows his connection with it. The court in any event can always order the prosecution of any director or other officer, or indeed of promoters, managers or shareholders.

A receiver must not be confused with the Official Receiver. A receiver is appointed by a secured creditor, in other words the owner or proprietor of a mortgage or debenture, to sell the assets of the company which are the subject of the charge, for the purpose of repaying moneys due to him. If there is a debenture which gives a general charge on the assets and undertaking of the company, the receiver is given the power to act as manager, for the purpose of running the business whilst carrying out a programme of realization.

A receiver, once appointed, deals with the directors who remain in office, although the powers of the board to conduct business are vested in the receiver, until such time as he is paid out or the company wound up. However, the appointment of a receiver is an act of insolvency and in most cases the company goes into voluntary or compulsory liquidation when the directors are superseded. In rare cases, a receiver may carry on and may succeed in realizing funds to pay off the debenture, when the directors will resume normal working. Of course, where a director performs an executive function the receiver may well be bound to continue to employ and pay him as an executive. The wages of employees are a preferential charge in such cases. The receiver may call upon the directors for a statement of affairs, and may also call upon the secretary to confirm his concurrence by counter-signature.

In Scotland, unlike England, a receiver did not formerly have powers of management to continue the business. The action of the Upper Clyde shipbuilders, who staged a 'work-in' to save their jobs and salvage the business, highlighted this discrepancy as against English law. This was rectified in 1972, but in general the position within the European Economic Community is that there are no receivership systems to enable creditors to realize on a going-concern basis.

The liquidator, or a receiver in appropriate cases, can call upon the shareholders who have not paid for their shares in full or who have got the shares without proper consideration to pay the balance due. Furthermore, there are provisions, in cases in which shareholders have transferred shares within the year prior to the commencement of the liquidation, to make the former owners pay instead. In the case of unlimited companies these rules are of more general significance since the shareholders are jointly and severally liable to calls for the entire deficiency of the company. A director of an unlimited company who has no shares has, however, no liability. A former shareholder of an unlimited company has no liability after the lapse of two years from transfer. This can be contrasted with the continuing liability of a former partner for negligence which can last for many years.

One recent development has been for major companies, or companies dealing with a product in which there is some special interest, to be rescued from winding-up by Government action which has often led to complicated reconstruction transactions. A further development is the Industrial Common Ownership Act 1976 which might be utilized in place of winding-up, particularly when the shareholders' funds have been lost, but when the shareholders, under the influence of the board are prepared to co-operate—perhaps because of the chance of salvaging loans or minimizing liabilities on personal guarantees. It seems that if the company amends its objects then, subject to re-registration, it will qualify for a Government grant so that the industrial enterprise would continue. Such objects might

be to limit membership to employees who would have equal voting
rights; control by a majority of the employees working for it; provision
for profits similarly to be shared, and that, upon winding-up, the
assets remaining should go to another common ownership enterprise
or a central fund for the benefit of such enterprises as may be decided
by the members, or for charity.

Chapter 12

Partnerships, unlimited companies, operating agreements and nominees

It is important for a director to realize that, as a director, he has no liability, not even for the debts of an unlimited company, so long as he has behaved in accordance with his legal obligations. On the other hand, in a partnership each partner is jointly and separately liable for all the obligations of the partnership firm. Even though he may be only a salaried partner with no interests in capital or profits, a partner whose name appears on the letterheading or in the particular file at the Business Names Registry is liable to contribute to, or pay the entirety of, the debts in the firm due to outsiders. For what it may be worth, however, a salaried partner may have a right of indemnity against profit-sharing partners.

Under the new rules introduced as part of the fundamental laws of the European Economic Community, an incorporated company has to state its registered number in the letterheading. It is therefore easier to distinguish between partnerships and unlimited companies. There was previously an anomaly in the law, in that, as long as the names of all the directors appeared on the letterheading of an unlimited company, there was no necessity to state that the names appeared as directors rather than partners. The unlimited company has been used primarily as a means of incorporating professional firms whose profession, unlike that of solicitors and chartered accountants, permitted this. In order to avoid the requirement introduced in 1967 that all private limited companies should file their annual report and accounts, a few companies did choose to become unlimited. Under the new rules a private unlimited company can re-register as a public limited company.

An 'operating agreement' is the term sometimes used to describe a contract between shareholders of a private company, as to the way in which various matters should be dealt with between them. On the face of it these matters could well be set out in the Articles of Association, but for reasons of privacy or informality it is sometimes preferred to have such an agreement. These may well be lengthy documents. They may regulate the provision of moneys, and the way assets are to be dealt with. They may define obligations between shareholders in terms that are commercial and direct, rather than those set out in words and clauses in Articles of Association. One particular subject of an operating agreement is the way in which one party may buy out the other, or may bring the association to an end, and avoid being locked in as a minority shareholder who has no directorship. Such agreements normally also deal with the rights of parties to be, or to nominate and remove, representative directors. Agreements such as these, backing up arrangements for private companies, can be called quasi-partnerships.

Nominees are frequently used to hold shares, and the right to have and change nominee shareholders in private companies is frequently set out in an operating agreement. With public companies, the position of nominees has always been the subject of some concern. It has led to rules, in cases of companies which have a quotation on a recognized stock exchange, that the owner of 5 per cent or more in nominal value of any class of shares which carry unrestricted voting rights, must disclose his identity and give notice of all dealings in the shares of the company. While he has at least such a holding, particulars have to be kept in a register, open to inspection by members and the public in the same way as the register of directors' interests. A similar rule is imposed on all companies holding shares to a nominal value in excess of one tenth of any class, to include in its accounts the name and nature of the holding. If the company has many such holdings and the directors are of the opinion that it would result in particulars of excessive length, these can be omitted from the accounts, but must still be included in a statement accompanying the annual return to be filed at the Companies Registry.

Arising from the use or abuse of nominees and the difficulties that would arise from prohibition, the period for notice was reduced from fourteen to five days, and the level for compulsory disclosure of interests was reduced from 10 per cent to 5 with effect from 18 April 1977, and powers conferred to enable the board of directors to require particulars of true beneficial ownership and voting agreements. Because of this, quite apart from the obligation on a holder of 5 per cent or more to give notice, directors have been given a power to enquire. Any holder may be required by the board to disclose whether he is the beneficial owner and if not who, so far as he is aware, has an interest in voting shares of a public company which are quoted. A holder must also disclose on enquiry whether he has any voting agreements or an arrangement. Information so obtained by the board should be recorded in a separate part of the share register. Failure to disclose, unless the Articles so provide, does not deprive the holder of his voting rights, whatever criminal liability that may be involved, and frivolous or vexatious enquiries need not be answered. The Minister can grant exemption after consultation with the Governor of the Bank of England if there are special reasons. The Secretary of State has power by statutory instrument to prescribe a lower percentage. Since then, someone who had between 5 and 10 per cent has been obliged to give notice following this change of his interest in such a nominee holding. Further, whenever there is a change in his own holding which leaves him with more than 5 per cent, he must similarly give notice. Under the listing agreement, a public quoted company, as soon as it is notified of a 5 per cent holding, must pass the information on to the Stock Exchange. Here it is regarded as vital market information, and will help directors to discover the real identity of the owner of such holdings.

The use of nominees to cloak in secrecy the activities of operators on the Stock Exchange dealing in the shares of public companies has been the subject of legislation proposals, in particular 'warehousing'. This is an operation in which financial organizations friendly to the operator will build up holdings in the selected public company in their own or nominee names and then deal with those holdings in line with what the operator wants. In one way or another they share in the profits or losses so made. The problems of barring these arrangements is that any solution tends to restrict innocent and proper activities in a free market.

Further, any disclosure made to the board of the identity behind a nominee purchaser ought to be notified immediately to the Stock Exchange in accordance with the rules of the listing agreement and not left over to the annual return and accounts. The view of the Share and Loan Department seems to be that such information is always important to the market and therefore price sensitive. A special Bank of England nominee company to cloak royalty, heads of state and other special holders has been exempted from the disclosure obligations by regulation. Stockjobbers are also exempted. One concession made since 18 April 1977 concerns the obligation to give notice of dealings in important shareholdings. These are holdings which exceed 5 per cent, in a class of shares which have unrestricted voting rights, and they have been qualified so that minor dealings which do not move the holding up or down into a different whole number percentage are no longer notifiable. Figures are calculated by rounding down to the nearest whole number. On the other hand a group of companies (ie a company and its subsidiaries) is to be treated as one for the purpose of calculating whether 5 or more per cent is held, and directors should give notice accordingly. In addition the private interests of directors, otherwise concealed or confused through nominee or trustee holdings are the subject of the new disclosure rules and companies are required under the listing agreement to give immediate notification to the Quotations Department of the Stock Exchange for publication—leaving it to the following day, as allowed under the statute, is not good enough.

Difficulty has been experienced with overseas purchasers who are not themselves subject to United Kingdom law. It has been argued that since the statutes have not been expressed in terms to bind foreign nominees foreign nominees need not comply, even though the true owner is in the United Kingdom and such an owner would only be liable to give notice if he has acquired more than 5 per cent.

Chapter 13

The directorship

It must be appreciated that the description 'company director' may apply to a number of related but not necessarily identical functions.

In origin the directors were the supervisors, in some sense the trustees for the shareholders, and were paid a fee for this service. Today, a directorship has come to be the appropriate status for a senior executive or manager, to such an extent that many boards of directors are composed either exclusively of wholetime directors of the company or its group, or professional directors who combine professional services to the company with a seat on the board. However, it is still common for public companies to have outside directors and appointment of non-executive directors is being encouraged.

An undischarged bankrupt may not serve as a director, nor a person in respect of whom the court has made an order banning such an appointment. Such an order is not effective for more than five years, and usually arises from some offence under company law. A person may also be disqualified for persistent registration defaults. Otherwise, anyone capable of acting may be appointed, except a person who has attained the age of seventy years, in which case his appointment must be approved in general meeting after special notice has been given stating his age. Once appointed a director must obtain his share qualification if the Articles of the company require that a director have a minimum shareholding, but otherwise a director does not also have to be a shareholder. If, where a minimum shareholding is required, a director fails within two months, or such shorter time as the Articles provide, to be registered as a shareholder, he vacates office by law, and cannot be re-appointed until he is registered. Usually the Articles also provide that if a director ceases to hold the minimum shareholding he ceases to be a director.

There are stricter rules for public companies. Here directors must sign a consent to be appointed before being named either in the Articles or in the prospectus documents, and in addition must make arrangements to pay for any qualification shares. With all companies, whether on incorporation or on a change of directorship, the notification to the Registrar of Companies must contain a consent by that person to act in that capacity. The same rule applies to secretaries.

Appointment and emoluments

Appointment as a director is in one of three ways:

(a) upon incorporation, as a result of being named in the Articles or in a memorandum, appointing the first directors, by the signatories to whom this power is given by the incorporation documents;

(b) by election to the board by a resolution of the members of the company, or of a class entitled to representative directors. The class members need not themselves be shareholders but could be loan stock holders or even a trade union, if so allowed by the Articles; or

(c) by invitation from the board. Usually the Articles allow the directors to fill casual vacancies or appoint additional directors up to the maximum number fixed by the Articles. Any new member so appointed, or after retiring by rotation, has to come up for re-election by the members at the next annual general meeting.

Strange as it may seem, at one time any person could be appointed a
director of a company, and no formal consent was necessary. There
were cases where well-known personalities had been appointed as
directors without their knowledge. Upon objection, they were treated
as renouncing and not resigning office, although according to the
statutes they were directors, with all the duties of directors, until they
resigned.

Directors are not entitled to any payment for services as such unless
this is provided for in the Articles of Association. They do however
have the same right as any employee at common law to claim
reimbursement for expenses properly incurred in the course of
discharging their duties. Sometimes the Articles lay down an annual
fee, sometimes shareholders are asked specifically to vote a fee to the
directors, but payment is a matter of internal management to be
settled by the board. When shareholders are asked to vote a fee, the
item appears in the accounts for the company to be approved at the
annual general meeting. The accounts, or a statement attached to
them, have to set out not only the amount of remuneration but also all
emoluments from all the company's resources. This expression is
much wider than fees or salary, and includes the value of all benefits in
kind. The amount of pensions and the amount of compensation for
loss of office paid to directors, both past and present, must be given.
These rules take account, in the definition of directors, of those who
hold executive positions with the firm or who held such positions
before becoming directors. The fixing of a payment to directors for
purely supervisory functions, or for direct employment with the
company, is a matter for the board.

It will be appreciated that whilst shareholders can obtain full
particulars of the terms of any service contracts where directors are
employed, the cost to the company is only given in the accounts in
terms of totals. In 1967, more for government statistical purposes than
for the benefit of the shareholders, rules were introduced setting out
the information as to remuneration which it is the obligation of all
companies to disclose in the accounts. There is no distinction, so far as
employment terms are concerned, between a director and any other
employee, although the position of managing director is usually the

subject of a special provision in the Articles, and these have to be looked at in each case. A managing director holds office subject to any contract with him, and is usually not liable to retire by rotation. He has the powers conferred on him by the board, as they think fit, and these can be altered or withdrawn by changes in the Articles, whatever the existing Articles may say. Nevertheless if a director is to have a long term contract or contracts of employment or even a consultancy agreement or similar arrangement for services as an independent contractor for more than five years at a time, the agreement must first be approved by the shareholders in general meeting. This does not affect long term service agreements already operative at the time the 1980 Act takes effect. The new principle also catches agreements with firms or companies of which a director is a member or which are owned or controlled by a director. If not so approved then legally the employment is liable to termination by reasonable notice not exceeding six months and any term of the agreement which contravenes the prohibition is void.

There are certain restrictions on the benefits which may be received by directors. Unless it results from a contract made prior to 1946, they may not be paid a tax-free salary; all contracts are to be treated as gross amounts before taxation. Payments for compensation for loss of office, or for retirement, must be disclosed to shareholders and approved by them. Furthermore, where compensation is payable on the disposal of the business or part of the business of the company, or in connection with a transfer of shares, the director holds the money on trust for the company unless the transaction is disclosed to and approved by the members. In particular, in the case of a take-over bid, these details ought to be included in any notice of the offer given to members.

Loans to and finance for directors

As a general principle loans or credit facilities for directors have been restricted as undesirable. The approach is that directors would do better to devote their energies to raising loans for themselves rather than try to divert assets of the company to personal use. Since 1967, except where loans were made to enable a director to pay expenditure (incurred as part of his duties and to be repaid if not approved by the next annual general meeting) or by companies whose business was moneylending or the giving of guarantees, loans by limited companies were prohibited. The prohibition did not apply to loans made to employees who were not directors of the company or its subsidiary or holding company before they became directors. Under the new rules of the 1980 Act the prohibitions remain the same but the scope has been extended to catch transactions intended to avoid the general prohibition. In particular the rules have been extended to catch what are called quasi-loans in the case of public companies and private companies associated with them. These are transactions under which a third party pays the original liability on the basis that the company will pay him or see that the third party is paid. There is a further extension designed to catch credit transactions under which such a company pays or gives a guarantee or security for payment in return for the supply or hire of goods, or the leasing of land. Elaborate anti-avoidance provisions have been enacted, particularly the provision which makes a director not only indemnify the company but also account for any gain. The general effect of these provisions is to allow only certain exceptions in favour of a director as follows:

(a) quasi-loans or credit transactions which do not exceed £5,000 in total;
(b) funds provided by a company to reimburse expenditure incurred by a director or to avoid such expenditure not exceeding £10,000 in total;
(c) transactions by moneylending companies (other than a recognized bank) by way of loan, quasi-loan or guarantee not exceeding £50,000 in total; and
(d) housing loans made by a moneylending company which does not exceed £50,000 in total.

It is considered, however, that employee share schemes are also excepted so long as these have been approved by the company in general meeting. It should be noted however that payments or advances made for the purpose of defraying expenses incurred by directors as agents of the company are not caught by any of the prohibitions, as these are not personal liabilities of the director. They do not, therefore, call for reimbursement by the director and do not amount to a provision of credit for the personal benefit of the director. For example, the use by a director of a credit card in the name of the company and in connection with the company's business will not be within the mischief which these rules anticipate and are directed against. On the other hand use of such a credit card for personal items could constitute an offence. However this could come within the exemption for quasi-loans so long as it is clear that the director is bound to reimburse the payment within two months and the total of the quasi-loans outstanding to that director does not exceed £1,000. Again, the prohibitions against loans or guarantees or security by public companies and private companies associated with them to or for persons connected with directors does not apply where the amount involved is not more than £5,000 or is in the ordinary course of business and on normal (and not more favourable) terms. The rules governing loans to and finance for directors have been drawn in complex style for public protection and directors seeking financial support from their company should seek legal advice on the particular facts.

Election and retirement by rotation

Rotation of directors, whereby they come up in turn for re-election at the annual general meeting every three years, is standard practice for public companies in order that shareholders may secure some nominal control over the board, and is something upon which the Stock Exchange is insistent. Many private companies, particularly those where the directors and shareholders are substantially the same, exclude these provisions as a nuisance and a trap for the unwary. Quite a few private companies have been found to have their entire board technically out of office for not observing this provision in the Articles! There are detailed provisions to establish whose turn it is to form part of the one third which should be re-elected in any year. Directors who have been appointed by the board during the year have to be re-elected at the annual general meeting. Each director should be voted upon individually. Managing and executive directors are usually exempt from retirement by rotation.

Dismissal from office and compensation

A director, once appointed, holds office under the Articles of Association as a matter of law. In the first instance, whatever the Articles of Association may provide, by law a director may always be removed from office by a resolution of members passed by a simple majority, so long as the twenty-eight days' special notice to propose removal is given. Furthermore, a director may also be removed from office by special resolution, notice for which can be waived by the holders of 95 per cent of the voting shares agreeing. In both cases a director may be able to recover damages for unfair dismissal, but he is nevertheless removed. Only if the director has an agreement as such with the shareholders, under which the proposed removal is a breach, might he get an injunction to restrain his removal.

It has been established that if the Articles provide for a particular share to have special voting rights on a resolution to remove a director, such rights can also be used to stop the removal of a director. As will be appreciated, this involves complicated provisions which require technical expertise. What is more important is that the director should bear in mind, if he has been employed as a director with a special function, that it is implied that his employment comes to an end if he ceases to be a director in consequence of a resolution by shareholders. The agreement should provide in some way that, if employment is terminated as a result of his ceasing to be a director, this is without prejudice to a right to compensation, including his rights under the appropriate employment legislation for mediation and compensation for unfair dismissal.

No director can be appointed for life, although a director so appointed before 1946 cannot be removed. This exception must now be almost academic as there is a rule that directorships cannot be assigned. It is therefore unlikely that there will be any case in which it would be effective.

A threat of removal under the special notice procedure does give a director certain rights. As soon as notice of an intended resolution for removal is given to the company it must send a copy to the director. The director can then make representations in writing—so long as they are of reasonable length!—and can require that members should receive, with the notice of the resolution, a statement that his representations have been made and that a copy has been sent to every member. If the representations are received too late, or the company is at fault in circulating them, the director may require that these shall be read out to the meeting without prejudice to his right to be heard orally. Provision is made that these representations need not be sent out or read if someone satisfies a court that they are defamatory.

Removal in this way does not deprive a person from compensation or damages payable to him in respect of the termination of his appointment, or of any other appointment terminating with the directorship.

The Articles usually provide for termination of a directorship in other varying circumstances—apart from death, failure to hold qualification shares, a shareholders' resolution, or an order of the court that a person is not to be a director. These circumstances arise if the director:

(a) becomes bankrupt or makes a composition with his creditors;
(b) becomes of unsound mind;
(c) **resigns by notice in writing to the company**; or
(d) is absent from meetings of directors for more than six months without permission of the directors.

It is not unusual to find a provision that a director shall cease to be a member of the board, if called upon by all or by a majority of his colleagues to resign. Such a provision is particularly useful, or dangerous according to your viewpoint, with public companies where there is a clash of views in the boardroom. Intransigent directors—in one case at least it has been the chairman—are quietly removed without need to inform or involve the shareholders and the public. Once again, in the absence of a well drawn-up service contract a director may find himself without any right to compensation.

There are two aspects to the question of compensation for loss of a directorship: the basis on which it should be computed, and the way in which it is to be taxed. So far as professional advisers are concerned in dealing with these issues, the tendency is to look at the position as a whole in order to achieve the most beneficial result for the individual.

The right of a director, if he also holds an executive position like any other employee, is to be compensated for wrongful or unfair dismissal contrary to the terms of his contract of employment. By statute an employee is entitled to compensation subject to a formula, if he has been unfairly dismissed. The figure is made up of compensation, plus an additional sum if reinstatement is ordered but not given. In any hearing before the Industrial Relations Tribunal the burden of proof is on the employer. This should be a much quicker procedure than a formal legal court action for wrongful dismissal. It must also be noted that proceedings for unfair dismissal should be brought within three months of the effective date of termination although there is a discretion to allow an extension of time if it was not reasonably practicable for the complaint to be made in that time. An employer can avoid liability for unfair dismissal if the reason was redundancy! Accordingly, except where the facts are reasonably clear, it is always as well to claim not only on the basis of unfair dismissal, but also for the alternative statutory compensation for redundancy. Where there is redundancy, once again the employer has to disclose his position, and the director's solicitors can still advise on a wrongful dismissal claim.

On a claim for wrongful dismissal, an executive director can claim to be compensated for the loss of the remuneration he would have earned under his contract, but he is at the same time under a duty to seek other reasonable employment. Once such employment is obtained the claim can only be measured, apart from the gap between jobs, by the difference, if any, in the pay and emoluments. Not unreasonably, in calculating the damages, any statutory award for unfair dismissal or redundancy must be brought into account. Agency fees properly paid to obtain new employment can be added to the amount of the damages. Attempts by the director to obtain new employment are expected to take time, so that compensation is likely to amount to anything from three months to two years' salary, in some cases even more, where a director is near the end of his working life and re-engagement difficult to achieve.

The taxation rule that is basic to the position is that compensation up to a fixed amount is not liable to tax, but any excess is treated as the income of the year in which it is received, unless the income represents a specific period which had accrued due but had to be recovered in the action, for example a commission on profit for a previous year which should have been paid earlier but which had been withheld.

It seems that a testimonial present made by an employer *ex gratia* without any contractual liability, so long as it is a proper payment for the company, may also escape tax, for instance the gold watch or colour television set to mark long employment, or the silver salver with a purse of £500 to mark appreciation of the standards set by the editor of a newspaper on his retirement.

Retirement and pensions

Retirement and death are the normal ways for a directorship to come to an end, and each of these have consequences. So far as retirement is concerned, it may merely be a polite way of bringing hostilities to an end, and may occasionally be coupled with compensation payments. On the other hand it can be as a result of reaching the retirement age or a breakdown of health. Many companies run pension schemes either funded with trustees, or by means of an insurance company scheme, so that the payments are not made out of the resources of the company. It was not uncommon, particularly where directors were controlling directors for tax purposes, that is to say having more than 5 per cent of the shares or of the voting shares, for the company to undertake in the contract of employment to pay a pension; or for the company to propose to pay a pension even though there was no direct obligation on it to do so. In such cases the Revenue subjected the matter to scrutiny, but were usually prepared to allow a pension based on not more than two-thirds of salary at retirement or averaged on recent preceding years as a reasonable payment to be made out of the profits of the company before corporation tax. Now it is possible, and indeed advisable, for such pensions to be funded with insurance policies. The salary must not have been artificially increased for the sake of the formula. In so far as the Revenue will not agree in any particular case, the pension if paid will have to be paid out of profits remaining after corporation tax. It is sometimes the practice, instead of paying a pension, to pay a consultancy fee, particularly if the retiring director has expert knowledge. This will be earned income and a charge on the company's income before corporation tax is levied. If such an agreement is to last for more than five years, it will now have to be approved by the company in general meeting. Since agreements of this kind are frequently expressed to be for life, this must be borne in mind. Whole-time working directors are treated in the same way as other staff for the purpose of being eligible for any staff pension scheme. At one time, once such a director held more than 5 per cent he had to come out of the scheme, but remained entitled to benefits accrued up to that date; all wholetime directors may be in such a scheme.

Loss of pension benefits are a proper item for compensation on wrongful or unfair dismissal, and pension schemes contain directions for trustees to deprive of benefits employees who leave the service of the company, often in penal terms when employment is terminated for good cause.

Pension schemes should allow employees who leave the company service by mutual agreement to keep or even to transfer accrued rights, but this varies so much in practice that each scheme must be examined. A director considering a change of employment ought to examine any pension scheme and take advice on it, especially if his accrued rights are of substantial value.

In recent years the Inland Revenue have been prepared to include what is called dynamism in pension fund schemes. This is to allow pensions to increase after retirement by reference to the cost-of-living index. It is understood that the principle was conceded originally for civil service pensions. For those commercial companies which can afford to pay the additional premiums involved on their own account, and for their employees by providing the additional remuneration so that the employee can make his contribution, this may well be worth while. This is particularly the case with whole-time working directors who are in high tax brackets. In the Finance Act 1973, provision was made to allow directors with more than 5 per cent of the shares to qualify for membership of the pension schemes of the companies which employ them, and for all such working directors this is a most important concession on which they should now take advice.

Most pension schemes, and indeed contracts providing for retirement annuities, will contain provisions for widows and dependants. These require examination both on joining a company and on leaving it. It is sufficient to note these provisions are the significant factors, which ought to be taken into account in considering and taking advice upon whether to leave or stay with a company. It is also important, in the creation of any pension scheme by a company, to make certain that the Memorandum of Association of the company expressly permits the payment of pensions to directors. Most companies incorporated on standard forms after 1948, when pension fund schemes became more general, usually include this, but it must be checked. Since the relationship between the director and the company in some part is founded on the laws of trusts, unless there is express power in the Memorandum the director is not entitled to receive, nor the company to pay, the pension. However, if a bad case arose the courts might try to ameliorate the effect of this apparently strict rule.

Expense accounts

Expense accounts have been the subject of much imaginative
embroidery, and in consequence the Revenue have introduced
salutary rules intended to avoid taxable profits being eroded. For this
reason a special return of expenses and emoluments is required for all
employees earning more than a prescribed annual salary. Special rules
are also applied to cars run or provided at the expense of the firm.

Even benefits for wives are subject to scrutiny, and much ingenuity
has been devoted to establishing that the expenses of a wife
accompanying her husband on a business trip ought to be allowed for
taxation purposes, and not treated as additional remuneration. It is
not a case today of secretaries, whose expenses will be allowed,
masquerading as wives, but rather of wives pretending to be
secretaries!

New, stringent rules have been introduced for directors and higher
paid employees of all commercial companies to tax benefits in kind
such as the use of a company car, executive clothes, cheap loans,
medical treatment and indeed any benefit provided by reason of
employment to them or members of their family. These new rules are
extremely complex and in practice the Inland Revenue will have to
rely on the audit of the company to extract the information so that
assessments can be made on the individual, and legal advice may be
required on interpretation.

It will be readily appreciated, however, that, depending on the
particular facts, taxation of a personal benefit will be unlikely to
produce a total cost to the director equivalent to the expense of
providing that benefit himself. Care has to be taken to establish
whether in a particular case the arrangements are not caught by the
extended restrictions (as in the case of public companies and private
companies associated with them) prohibiting credit transactions for
directors.

Chapter 14

The director as a member of the staff

A director is only entitled to fees for his services as such; but it is common for directors, even when they are the owners of most of the shares in a private company, to treat themselves as executive directors. A director who is not an owner of the business is often appointed in the first place to be works director or sales director, or perhaps employed as works manager and at the same time or later, appointed to the board. What has to be considered is the contract of employment which governs the position in law between such an employee and the company. A person who is employed as a working director holds the office and in turn the employment, and is subject to the Articles of Association. All Articles contain provisions to remove directors by resolution of the shareholders, and some also allow removal by

decision of the board. It is an implied term of holding office as a
director that he is subject to this summary termination. It is important
to a director to clarify this point. His position is different if he is
employed as a manager, who is entitled to be a member of the board
during employment. Removal from the board does not break the
contract, although it may be that such treatment will entitle the person
to repudiate the entire contract if reinstatement is refused, and to
claim damages, but each case turns on its exact facts. Notice must now
be a minimum of one week for termination during the first year (so
long as employment has lasted four weeks) and then one week
additional for each year worked up to twelve years.

In this connection a director who is also employed as an executive
should also bear in mind that, like any other employee, if an
appointment is not renewed after more than 104 weeks of employment
there may be a right to compensation so long as it has not been
excluded by a contract for a term of more than two years. There is also
the right to notice, or payment instead, as follows:

after twelve years—not less than twelve weeks;
two to twelve years—not less than one week for each year
employed;
four weeks up to two years—one week.

Unless shareholders approve the service agreement in general meeting
the company cannot contract for employment of a director by the
company or a subsidiary for more than five years at a time. Contracts
must be capable of termination by notice not limited to misconduct or
other specified circumstances. For the resolution to be valid a
memorandum setting out the terms must be available for inspection at
the registered office for fifteen days prior to and at the meeting. To the
extent (but not further) that this is not observed, the contract is void
and is deemed to be capable of termination at any time on reasonable
notice. A working director is entitled to the normal full
statement under the Contracts of Employment Act if his service
agreement does not set out all the terms. These include entitlement to
holidays, including public holidays, the right to belong to a trade

union and the procedure for redress of grievances. So far as a director is concerned it is to be expected that this procedure will consist of an application to the chairman, followed by a reference to the board as a whole, or perhaps to private arbitration.

If the duties of the director are merely to attend board meetings, then it seems he is not an employee within the meaning of the protective legislation. On the other hand, if the director works for the company, even only part-time, he may still be entitled to be treated as an employee and so have rights to claim, within the regulations, for redundancy or unfair dismissal.

Industrial relations

Under the employment protection legislation companies have to disclose, for the purpose of collective bargaining with trade unions, all information about their business without which trade union representatives would be impeded in collective bargaining, and all information which it would be in accordance with good industrial relations practice to disclose for such bargaining. A code lays down guidelines on this. The company need not produce original documents or allow copies to be made, except documents actually passing the information on to the union, nor does the company have to assemble or compile information when this would involve work or expenditure out of all proportion to the value of the information.

In concluding collective bargaining, if a director or other person, in furnishing any such information, either deliberately or carelessly makes an untruthful statement or produces inaccurate or incomplete documents, he commits an offence. It is therefore important for directors to check the accuracy of information which is given in relation to the accounts with the auditors. Similarly, summaries of agreements and legal documents ought to be referred to the company's solicitors to confirm the correctness of the interpretation. In some cases, particularly where solicitors were not concerned in the preparation of the original documents, the board could have one or two surprises in the course of such an exercise.

Trade unions

Trade unions are to be considered by directors as bodies which in law
have their own special status, apart from their members and their
representatives within the company. Under the law, trade unions can
sue or be sued, although the question of whether or not an action
should be brought against a trade union requires most careful advice
on the position in each case. Generally speaking, a trade union will
have its own professional organizers by whom the staff of the firm may
wish to be represented. Indeed, it is the right of any employee
involved in a dispute with his employer to be represented by his own
union—and no union can insist on representing an employee to the
exclusion of another union. A director should accept and recognize
that such a representative is an expert, and ought to be treated as such.
Among trade unions great play is often made of the desire to exclude
lawyers—with their meticulous attention to detail and precise usage of
words—from trade union negotiations with workmen unversed in the
law. Nonetheless, the trade unions' official representatives are usually
highly skilled negotiators in the specialized field, and experienced
orators and advocates. Directors of smaller companies who attempt to
deal with them without legal advice may well be at a grave
disadvantage, unless they can in turn call in some representation from
an employers' organization or their own professional advisers. The
cost of such cases can be heavy for small firms and there is a growing
market for legal costs insurance of businesses.

   Such business matters should be distinguished from normal staff
representation within the firm which, except in the case of large firms,
is unlikely to involve anyone other than employees who select some
member of the staff to speak for them. The subject of industrial
relations as such has undergone much change as a result of recent
legislation. Traditional attitudes can no longer prevail. In all but the
simplest questions, whilst it is not necessarily the case that legal
guidance should be sought, as a general rule, directors would be well
advised to consider whether the problems in hand should not be
reviewed with the solicitors to the company.

Individual directors also have to consider their own rights and increasingly, technical directors at least, are becoming members of unions. This is a means of seeking protection in relation to employer companies of which they are not shareholders, or which are so large that any shareholding is insignificant. This is the right of an executive director as a matter of law in any event.

Restrictive covenants and know-how

The individual director is often faced in his employment with special obligations to preserve the secrets of the firm and not to compete or make special skills available to competitors. These restrictive covenants are frequently so worded as to be unfair when examined from the point of view of the employee. Whilst an employee may wish to seek the protection of a trade union and guidance as to what is the union policy to accept, it is important to appreciate that the English courts, as a matter of public policy, exercise a strict control against enforcing covenants which are unreasonable. A distinction is drawn between obligations where a man is selling a business with goodwill, and a contract of employment. In this last class, the rule is that a man must be allowed to earn his living and use his skills. What is more, he is entitled to work in his own home town, and the courts are reluctant to agree that a man can be stopped from getting employment in an area for a period of years, which could be the result of the restrictive terms inserted in some contracts of employment. Generally speaking, the stricter the wording in a contract the greater the chance that the restrictions would be thrown out by the court as being over and beyond what is reasonable. If the contract is not carefully drawn up, the judge has only to find just one part of it unreasonable in this respect, and the whole of the restrictions may be ineffective. Accordingly, boards of directors in dealing with service agreements should not be too zealous in seeking specific protections on paper, as this may defeat their object. Furthermore, they should review existing contracts carefully as they come up for renewal, and take advice as to whether or not the restrictions are of any real value.

It does remain true even without covenants, as an implied term of any contract, that an executive director must not make use of special knowledge obtained as a director of, for example, secret processes. It is perfectly reasonable for a company to require promises to preserve secrets, not to take employees away, nor to use the firm's name or to claim some former association with the firm as a means of securing introductions for competition. Such cases depend on their facts, but a technical director employed to develop a particular process may be put under an obligation not to develop that process for someone else, nor to disclose the means of producing some item, Much information of this kind is of great value, but cannot be protected by registration as a patent or copyright, and this judges will recognize. The court will give effect to restrictions that are drafted reasonably and fairly to protect the ownership in this class of information, which is loosely but logically called 'know-how', but such drafting is a matter of special skill and advice.

Patents and copyright

In relation to patents and copyright, the law has special peculiarities, since a company cannot of itself invent or create anything. The legislation in respect of patents is intended to preserve monopoly rights for a period of time to enable the inventor to exploit the first fruits of his inspiration in relation to its practical application. There is no patent in ideas as such in the United Kingdom. Copyright is often confused with a registered design or trade mark. In respect of registered designs and trade marks there is no such limitation as to time, because the purpose is simply to record the right to a particular design or mark, as distinctive to the goods or services of the owner. Copyright is a right to restrain copying or exploitation, and is normally applicable to works of literature, music and art, although architects' designs and drawings are the subject of copyright and cannot be employed without payment. The work of employees acting in

accordance with the terms of their job can result in the creation of an
invention or the product of work which is capable of registration on
behalf or in the name of a company. As a normal rule where it is the
work of one man, the first registration will be sought in his name, and
he in turn will either assign it to the company or by deed acknowledge
that he holds it for the company. Sometimes, particularly when the
work is team-work and arises from research commissioned for the
company, the original application will be made to register in the name
of the company.

Both in relation to patents and copyrights, the method of
exploitation is either to sell or to grant rights for use, in exchange for a
periodic fee, which may either be a fixed amount payable by the year,
or calculated by reference to sales or shares of commission. There are
many ingenious ways of combining these types of provisions in the
licence granted. What is common is to find a condition as to variations
and improvements produced by the holder of the licence, which are to
belong to, or to be shared with or kept by the licence-holder as against
the owner of the original patent. Where a company is concerned it is
therefore important, if obligations are to be honoured, to ensure that
directors and staff are put under similar obligations. It has been said
that a director employed in design and research, whether or not it
appears in his contract, will be under an implied obligation to the
company to pass over for its benefit any invention made by him in
relation to the subject matter of his work. There is thus no problem in
such a case in respect of improvements on patents for which the
company is licensed. On the other hand, a sales or accounts director
may well have no such implied obligation. For this reason, in
America, whenever such work is handled by a company all directors
and staff are normally placed under contract with special terms to deal
with this situation. Where United Kingdom companies are licensed or
controlled by Americans employees are expected to accept such
special terms as routine. It is of course now easier to introduce express
conditions of this kind in the standard notice that has to be given
under the Contracts of Employment Act to all staff, including
directors. In the past, most engagements for jobs did not involve any

formal documentation, but with the new statutory machinery there should be no problem in arranging for advisers to prepare suitable clauses, though as a matter of good relations there would have to be consultations with existing staff first.

Licences held for the company

It is the practice, in relation to licences which are required for carrying on businesses, for a director to be named licensee and be responsible for the conduct of the business. In the case of the sale of liquor the rule is that a company cannot be a licensee and a manager upon the premises is made the licence-holder. This arises from the necessity to ensure good order. In the case of gaming licences or betting shop licences, there may be an individual, usually a director, as the licensee. But the company may in law hold a licence. The rules for each type of licence, whether it is to sell tobacco, to have music and dancing on the premises, or to carry on a slaughter house, may vary and each has to be considered separately, but wherever a director is named as the licence-holder it implies a special responsibility on his part to see that the business upon the premises is properly conducted. If it is not properly conducted, then that director may be personally liable to be punished at criminal law, in addition to the loss of the licence. A director who undertakes this responsibility is in a curious position because he is answerable not only for his own actions but also for those of the staff of the company. It is not unreasonable in such circumstances for a director who holds the licence to require to have the right to hire and fire the staff for which he is responsible, and indeed perhaps to require the company to indemnify him for acts and defaults of such staff. Again service contracts, because of this factor, ought to provide for termination of his job on loss of the licence, with payment in lieu of notice, the amount depending on whether he has himself been in default. A director who holds a licence on behalf of a company has to act as if he were a trustee of the benefit of the licence for the company, must only deal with it as the company directs, and must treat any value as the property of the company. It can be a disadvantage for a company itself to hold licences for several places of business because a loss of a licence at one place for some dereliction may result in all the licences being forfeit.

Chapter 15

Litigation, crime and penalties

In one sense there is no criminal offence that a company can commit, because it is itself a creature of the law. Since it only has an existence allowed to it by law it might be possible to argue that it has no capacity to do anything illegal. If this were assumed to be true then the company would always be innocent, and only the directors could be punished for wrong-doing! The law of companies has not developed in this way, although traces of this thinking can from time to time cause confusion. It is clear that a company is responsible for the acts of the board and of its servants in relation to its business. A company cannot appear in person in court and must be represented by counsel in the High Court, or by a solicitor in those courts where a solicitor has a right of audience.

A director cannot represent his company except in cases where the judge may give special authorization. He may give evidence for the company, but only a litigant appearing on behalf of himself, or a duly qualified lawyer, may discuss and argue the case in court. This rule does not apply outside the courts, where the company director or indeed the secretary may appear to represent the company before less formal tribunals. Because of the nature of a company as a person in law, it can be accused of conspiracy to defraud, or of producing fraudulent or misleading documents, and equally it can sue for defamation in relation to its business reputation. On the other hand, there must be at least two persons other than the company to establish a claim to a conspiracy to which the company is a third party.

As a general rule, the courts take the view that the company is responsible in damages at civil law for the wrongful actions of the board of directors who are managing the company, and of the wrongful actions of the managing or executive directors and other staff, when those actions occur in the course of management. It does not matter in this connection what the Memorandum and Articles of Association may provide. It is what has been done pursuant to such management. As for criminal offences, the company is similarly liable, even though the crime itself was outside the scope of the employment of the director or employee involved, as for example in the case of a transport company whose drivers exceed the permitted hours for continuous driving. Even if the activity is beyond the powers of the company, if the act committed was authorized by the board of directors the company may be liable in damages. If the resources of the company were responsible for the injury, it is fair that damages should be claimed against it. None of this 'vicarious liability' affects the possibility that the servant, or indeed the directors themselves, may also be liable in their personal capacity. On the other hand, since shareholders have in the ordinary way no management powers over a company, a company cannot be made liable for the wrong-doing of a shareholder in the civil or criminal courts.

All liability for a company is in reality based on the liability of a principal for an agent, or of a master for his servant. It follows that a company cannot be liable for anything done by shareholders or promoters before it was incorporated, although there are offences which promoters can commit, particularly in relation to false or inaccurate documents put into circulation before the company is incorporated. Since liability takes this form, if a director or other officer completes a document for which the company, because of some technicality, has no liability, then the director or other officer can be made personally liable. This is because he in effect held out that the document was correct, and intended others to act upon it.

Directors' vicarious responsibility

Directors, both civilly and criminally, have a special position. In the first place directors, as do other officers, have special responsibilities. Not only must they observe the rules governing the duties of directors themselves, but they must also see that their company complies with all the provisions of the Companies Acts. These provisions are imposed to balance the advantages that society has conferred upon companies by giving them a special status. In the course of this book, reference has been made to these various duties, but no special reference has been made to the penalties for disobedience. These are all summarized in the Table, which is based on one compiled for the Chartered Secretaries' Manual of Company Secretarial Practice and lists offences, the persons liable and the maximum penalty. It will be readily appreciated that this is not a definitive list of all possible offences by directors, but merely the crimes which can be committed under the Companies Acts. In addition, it should be appreciated that a director owes a duty of care. If he has been dishonest or unfair in the management of the company's affairs he may be liable in damages to the company. A director is only expected to act with such care as is reasonably to be expected, having regard to his own knowledge and experience. Part-time directors who fail to observe the wrong-doings of a managing director may escape liability. Again, directors are entitled, in the absence of dubious circumstances, to trust the company's accountants.

Executive directors on service contracts have a more onerous duty as they are usually under express obligations. If it is considered worth

while it may well be that a company will sue such a director for losses
suffered. The problem is, that unless the executive is bonded or
insured, it will not be worth while for a company to claim substantial
losses. The executive is unlikely to have sufficient resources to enable
him to pay the costs of a complex company claim, let alone the
damages! A director can however be made to account for profits made
by himself as a result of a breach of duty. The prudent company will,
in so far as is practical, insure against dishonesty on the part of
executives as well as their negligence in addition, where appropriate,
to product liability. This insurance should extend to the executive
directors and the company secretary.

Offences by directors and the company

Offences by the company and its directors, such as breaches of the
consumer credit regulations, or other crimes which arise mainly out of
breaches of economic codes of business conduct, fall either into the
category of cases where the company and its directors can be treated as
being party to the same offences, or those which are peculiar to the
company. For the latter special fines or penalties can be imposed.
Curiously, a company cannot be extinguished for a criminal offence,
but the Department of Trade has a power to apply to the court to wind
up a company in the public interest. It is unlikely that this power will
need to be used, as it is to be expected that by the time it pays its fines
and meets any civil damage claims, a company which commits
offences may well have become insolvent, if it was not already, and so
liable to be liquidated.

If the Secretary of State applies to court on the grounds of persistent
default in making returns, an order may be made prohibiting a person
from being a director or concerned with the management of
companies for up to five years from the date of the order. Persistent
default is proved by showing three or more defaults (whether or not on
the same occasion) but within the five years preceding the application.

This provision is made to apply to defaults in relation to overseas companies which are unregistered. Once an order is made, the court has to notify the Department of Trade, which maintains a register of such orders and any leave granted by the court, which will be deleted on expiry of the order.

While the Companies Acts nullify any provision in the Articles of Association or in any contract of employment indemnifying an officer or any person employed as auditor against liability for negligence, default, breach of duty or trust in relation to the company, this does not apply to offences against third parties. A board can therefore pay the expenses of defending any director (or employee for that matter) for any such breach in civil or criminal proceedings. It may in some circumstances be under an implied, if not an express obligation to do so where, for example, someone is the subject of allegations under the Health and Safety at Work legislation. Even in cases where it is a matter in relation to the company, an indemnity against expenses can be given where judgment is given in his favour, he is acquitted or, where although found to be wrong, the court makes an order granting relief on the basis that he had acted honestly and fairly and ought, in all the circumstances of the case, to be excused.

Reference has already been made to the special category of 'insider' dealing in shares and to the various prohibitions of behaviour as a director for which criminal sanctions may be invoked.

Offences by the staff

Offences by staff generally, apart from the special class of 'insider' offences on share dealings, may give rise to liability by the company as well, unless the directors can show that what has occurred was outside the normal activities authorized by them, in which case the company could not be held at fault. If the company was at fault, for example by having a vehicle on the road with defective brakes, it is liable to prosecution and in addition to claims in the civil court for damages which flow from such negligent acts.

Foreign representation

Foreign companies (that is incorporated outside Great Britain) are
allowed to carry on business in the United Kingdom, but if a place of
business is established, they are required to register with the
Companies Registry. If business is carried on in some name other than
its corporate name alone then the foreign corporation must also
register with the Registrar of Business Names in London or
Edinburgh and the return must be signed by a director or secretary or
any person responsible for management and filed within fourteen days
of commencing business. In the case of companies in business at 18
April 1977 or commencing within two months of that date registration
was supposed to have been effected by 18 July 1977. These overseas
companies must provide not only particulars of their constitution, and
a list and particulars of directors and secretary, but must also record
on the file the name and address of one or more persons resident in this
country, who can accept service of proceedings and notices on their
behalf. This does not restrict the conduct of proceedings against
companies which have not registered, but who maintain a place of
business in the United Kingdom. It seems likely that such a company
can be made party to proceedings by sending notice through the post.

Chapter 16

Insurance

A company, like any prudent business man, can insure itself not only against the loss or destruction of assets, but also against claims for damage whether caused by its business activities or by its employees and agents in the course of action undertaken in the interest of the company.

Whilst a company cannot for example drive a car, a director can, and damage caused by the director or any other employee in the course of company business will render the company liable for damage done.

Accident and third party insurance

As a general rule a company needs insurance not only in respect of accidents, but also in respect of all claims that may be made against it by other people. Because a company has limited liability, unless it is insured the person injured or who has suffered loss may be left without remedy, unless he can also sue a person in the employ of the company. The employee may in some cases have a right of indemnity from the employer, but it will be of no use if the company cannot meet the liability. A director, particularly of a small company, should always consider whether the company is fully insured against accidents. What is more important, he should make sure that the insurance company does not claim a right of re-imbursement in respect of claims by third parties from the employee who was at fault. This right of recourse, which many insurance policies now exclude, could have an odd result. Although the proprietor has taken out cover for the company, if he is involved in an accident whilst doing business for the company, he might find he was liable in law to pay back the compensation for which the insurers are liable to the victim.

There are many possible ways for a company to become involved in loss situations, and a director ought to make sure his company has fully comprehensive public liability cover, arranged through reputable brokers or agents. The loss of documents either in the custody of the company or in the post can prove a particular problem for companies in relation to share transfers or certificates. This is particularly the case if transfers have been stamped for transfer duty. It may prove difficult to convince the Inland Revenue of the loss. Accordingly cover for the reconstruction of lost documents and for documents lost in transit ought to be considered.

Another aspect of insurance arises in connection with protection against losses caused by dishonest employees. Quite often it is overlooked that one man's negligence may permit another man's dishonesty, and the insurance against negligence does not give any relief where the negligence was in supervision. Insurance against dishonesty commonly takes the form of a fidelity bond. Cashiers, managers handling cash, and accountants are usually highly trusted persons of good reputation, and employers frequently do not consider them to represent a serious risk. Nevertheless, the prudent board will effect such insurance, because a company can only act through its representatives and is thus always more vulnerable than the individual. The insurance proposal can be for large sums of money, and can involve quite extensive enquiries, which have been known to result in some quite surprising disclosures about the individuals concerned. On the other hand, many policies involve little more than the requirement of a written reference from previous employers.

Product insurance is of particular importance for companies engaged in export of goods or provision of services to foreign countries, in particular the United States. This is because of the concept of penal damages as a remedy. The specialist insurance brokers who have experience in this field may prove invaluable to a board not only in securing cover but advising how risks may be minimized.

Fire insurance

Fire and associated risks like explosion are a special class for insurance purposes, because they can not only cause damage to the insured's property but also injury to staff and customers on the premises. There is the risk of the spread of damage to adjoining property, or even burning down a whole neighbourhood. A fire may be accidental, or due to trespassers, or possibly to recklessness or carelessness by the company's staff. The rules about liability for the spread of fire are to a certain extent governed and restricted by statute, but a company should always carry its own insurance. Quite often a company occupies premises under a tenancy and the landlord is supposed to insure, but that policy does not cover the company's own furniture and fittings, nor does it give any cover for the disturbance of the business or the loss of profit that destruction can involve. Company directors should satisfy themselves that the company is fully and properly insured in respect of all aspects of its business premises. Due to inflation and the increase in replacement costs, particular care must be taken to review at least once a year all values for insurance purposes. In cases of partial or total destruction, directors should also consider whether it is likely to be economic to rebuild or whether their insurance cover should be for the cost of disturbance and relocation on a new site. In addition directors should consider whether rebuilding is permitted under planning and by-law regulations which contain waivers for existing but not replacement buildings.

Directors owe a duty of care to the company, and it may still be possible for a disappointed shareholder to sue the board of directors if the company suffers loss through not having the insurance that a reasonably prudent business man would effect in his own affairs. Furthermore, with the new rules concerning the validity of contracts entered into in breach of powers conferred upon the board by the Memorandum and Articles of Association, the directors and the secretary may well wish the company to carry insurance to indemnify the company, absolve them from liability in respect of claims by innocent third parties, and to provide them with independent legal representation in case of need.

The director's life—the insurable interest

Life assurance is inappropriate for companies in the ordinary way. It is based on payment by assurers on death, known as whole life assurance, or on survival for a period of years or earlier death, called endowment term assurance, or on death during a period of years only, called term insurance. Nevertheless, there is nothing to stop a company taking over a policy based on the life of a director or some other person for the purpose of financing. This device is sometimes used by a company in connection with a mortgage, as a means of providing for repayment of the mortgage after a period of years and on maturity of the policy. The director on whose life the policy is taken out is usually the youngest in order to obtain the lowest rate, but there is a substantial benefit to the company if the chosen director later drops dead. Assurance policies are of course also taken out to provide pensions or other benefits for directors.

Under term insurance, the insurer only pays if the life insured does not survive for the period of the policy. This type can be used by a company, apart from providing benefits for the widows, families and dependants of employees, to protect its interest in the life of an executive director whose death may cause commercial problems, such as a designer who may die while working on a project. It has even been known for a company to insure the life of a judge when the case was

going to last for many days, since the death of the presiding judge
means the court hearing having to start all over again! Term insurance
is also used to provide cover against the death of a director or some
other person who has lent money for working capital, and when the
company would be embarrassed to have to repay the money during a
period of expansion or development.

A company can take out insurance on the life of a director or an
executive for its own benefit where the company can be said to have an
insurable interest in his life. This means the company must have a
valid commercial interest in the continued life, and not merely that the
board considers that the insurance policy will be a good gamble.

From the point of view of the company, the value of a particular
director may be no more than the expense of the services of an
employment agency to find a replacement. However this can become
substantial where the director is skilled commercially, or is a
specialized technical director, since the services of a 'head-hunting'
agency to find a replacement, possibly by tempting him away from
some rival company, can be very expensive. It may well be that
companies should carry out personnel valuation, and at least take out
term insurance on the lives of such key staff. It might even be possible
in certain circumstances to insure, through Lloyd's underwriters,
against a director leaving, but generally term insurance can only be
against death or disability. Nevertheless, a company director who
knows and understands all that his work involves is an asset to the
shareholders, and ought perhaps to be insured for some value, if only
because he has managed to read this book!

Negligence insurance

As far as directors and secretaries are concerned, they are entitled to
look to the company in respect of all liabilities properly incurred by
them in the management of the business of the company, but not in
respect of wrongful acts committed by them. As already noted, the
contract of employment commonly contains an exemption or
indemnity clause covering any liability except negligence, default, or

breach of duty or trust in relation to the company.

Actions against directors for failure to show the standard of care owed by them are becoming more likely, particularly now that the law relating to actions by even minority shareholders acting in the name of the company against directors or officers has been liberalized. Professional directors, and the company secretary, may have special responsibilities. In view of this it may be thought judicious, particularly if by any chance there are circumstances involving American interests who might sue in the United States, to take out cover with insurers. It does not extend to fraud or dishonesty, criminal behaviour or suchlike, although the company can have separate fidelity insurance for its risks on the individuals it employs. This is not to be confused with legal costs insurance. Cover is on claims arising from breaches of duties owed to the company, errors, mistakes etc including breach of trust.

The cover can be arranged in the name of the company with indemnities to the extent of such insurance being given to the named individuals. It is true that there is power in the court, where an officer (or an auditor) has behaved honestly and reasonably and in all the circumstances (including those connected with his appointment) he ought fairly to be excused from liability for negligence, default, breach of duty or trust, to make an order accordingly. However, it may be prudent to seek insurance upon the basis that the premium cost may be kept down by virtue of this power in the court. In the past this power was thought to reduce very materially the chance of recovering worthwhile damages against auditors even if negligence was proved. Current experience suggests that this is not so effective and the secretaries of public companies may prove to be at the same high level of risk that auditors are, having regard to the circumstances now governing their appointment.

Legal costs insurance

This is a comparatively recent development in the United Kingdom and is intended to provide cover against the cost of litigation in case the insured becomes involved in disputes which are taken to court. Such cover might include insurance taken out by employers against claims by employees for wrongful dismissal. Care must be taken to make sure that the insurer allows the use of the company's own advisers, provided that they are competent, and does not seek to substitute the advisers selected by the insurer, who might control the situation in the interests of the insurer rather than the business.

Table I

This table is based upon one complied for the Chartered Secretaries' Manual of Company Secretarial Practice, which appears as Appendix 8 (Supplement No 5) in that Manual. It is reproduced here by permission of the Institute of Chartered Secretaries and Administrators, and includes additional references to the Companies Acts 1976 and 1980, which have been made by, and are the responsibility of, the publishers.

An alphabetical table of offences, with penalties

The penalties and offences listed here are primarily those contained in the Companies Acts, although there are numerous other offences which can be committed. The 'Companies Acts' as an expression is now defined to mean the Companies Acts 1948 to 1980. The following are now the relevant Acts included in this phrase:

The Companies Act 1948
The Companies Act 1967, Parts I and III
The Companies (Floating Charges and Receivers) (Scotland) Act
1972

The European Communities Act 1972, s 9
The Stock Exchange (Completion of Bargains) Act 1976, s 1 to 4
The Insolvency Act 1976, s 9
The Companies Act 1976
The Companies Act 1980

Directors should be aware that offences may be tried summarily in which event the powers of the magistrates on conviction if they pass sentence is restricted as against trial on indictment before a superior court such as a Crown Court where the presiding judge or judges have more extensive powers.

The statutory maximum fine referred to in the Table is defined by relation to ss 28 and 61 of the Criminal Law Act 1977, ie £1000 or whatever sum is fixed by order because of changing money values.

The 'default fine' is a penalty for each day during which the required action has not been taken after continual contravention. Unless the figure is given, under the Companies Act 1980, every officer who is in default is liable to a fine on conviction for which the maximum is one fiftieth of the statutory maximum per day ie £20 daily until the statutory maximum is changed.

An officer in default is any director or other officer who knows of the default and authorizes or permits the failure to do what the statute requires.

The first part of the Appendix lists offences during the ordinary 'life' of a company, and the second part deals with offences on winding up.

For ease of reference the following abbreviations are used:

UF: a fine unlimited as to amount;
SM: a fine not exceeding the statutory maximum;
SC: the maximum punishment that can be given on summary conviction;
I – the maximum punishment that can be given on conviction on indictment.

Part I—General Offences

SUBJECT MATTER OF OFFENCE	ACT AND SECTION	PERSONS LIABLE	MAXIMUM PENALTY
Accounts, failure to comply as to contents and form	1948 149(6)	Director	SC–£400 I–UF
Accounts, failure to give required details as to subsidiaries and not in annual return	1967 3(6)	Company and every officer	SC–1/5 SM or Default fine
Accounts, failure to give required details of holdings in other companies and not in annual return	1967 4(6)	Company and every officer	SC–1/5 SM or Default fine
Accounts, failure to comply with time limits to lay or deliver accounts, if necessary with English translation	1976 4	Director Company	SC–SM or Default fine
Accounts, failure to produce group accounts	1948 150(3) 1976 8	Director	I–UF SC–SM
Accounts, failure to send after demand	1948 158(3)	Company and every officer	SC–1/5 SM or Default fine
Accounts, failure to send to members or others 21 days before A.G.M.	1948 158(3)	Company and every officer	I–UF SC–SM
Accounts, failure to prepare or deliver accounts for overseas companies with English translation if necessary	1976 11	Company and every officer or agent	I–UF SC–SM or Default fine

SUBJECT MATTER OF OFFENCE	ACT AND SECTION	PERSONS LIABLE	MAXIMUM PENALTY
Accounts, failure to show certain corresponding items for the preceding year	1967 11(2)	Director	I–UF SC–SM
Accounts, false accounting	Theft Act 1968, s 18	Director, officer, manager	I–7 years or UF or both SC–6 months or SM or both
Allotment of shares or debentures before third day after prospectus issue	1948 50(3)	Company and every officer	I–2 years or UF or both SC–6 months or SM or both
Allotment of shares or debentures without shareholders' authority	1980 14(7)	Director	I–UF SC–SM
Allotment of shares with shareholders' authority, false statement to obtain authority	1980 18(6)	Any person	I–2 years or UF or both SC–6 months or SM or both
Allotments, failure to make return of	1948 52(3)	Every officer	I–UF SC–SM Default fine 1/10 SM
Allotments, contravention of procedure under ss 20–24, 26, 29 of 1980 Act	1980 30	Company and every officer	I–UF SC–SM
Allotment or offer of shares or debentures to public by private company	1980 15(3)	Company and every officer	I–UF SC–SM
Annual general meeting, failure to hold	1948 131(5)	Company and every officer	I–UF SC–SM
Annual general meeting, held under direction of Department of Trade, failure to notify resolution	1948 131(5)	Company and every officer	SC–1/5 SM or Default fine
Annual return, failure to complete and file	1948 126(2)	Company and every officer	SC–1/5 SM or Default fine

Offence	Statute	Who is liable	Penalty
Annual return, failure to make (with shares)	1948 124(3)	Company and every officer	SC–1/5 SM or Default fine
Annual return, failure to make (without shares)	1948 125(3)	Company and every officer	SC–1/5 SM or Default fine
Application for shares, failure to keep money in separate bank account	1948 51(3)	Company and every officer	I–UF SC–SM
Auditors, acting when disqualified or failing to give notice of vacating office	1976 13(6)	Any person	I–UF SC–SM or Default fine
Auditors, failure to notify Department of Trade that no auditors appointed or re-appointed or to notify removal to Registrar	1976 14(7)	Company and every officer	SC–1/5 SM or Default fine
Auditors, resignation, non-compliance with procedures	1976 16(7)	Company and every officer	I–UF SC–SM or Default fine
Auditors, misleading, false or deceptive statement in conveying information or explanation required by auditors	1976 19	Any officers	I–2 years or UF or both SC–6 months or SM or both
Balance sheet, circulation without profit and loss account and auditor's report annexed	1948 156(3)	Company and every officer	SC–1/5 SM
Balance sheets, circulation of unsigned	1948 155(3)	Company and every officer	SC–1/5 SM
Banking (and other) companies, failure to exhibit statement	1948 433(4)	Company and every officer	SC–1/5 SM or Default fine
Bankrupt, undischarged acting as director without leave of court	1948 187(1)	Bankrupt	I–2 years or UF or both SC–6 months or SM or both

SUBJECT MATTER OF OFFENCE	ACT AND SECTION	PERSONS LIABLE	MAXIMUM PENALTY
Bankrupt, undischarged acting as receiver or manager	1948 367(1)	Bankrupt	I–2 years or UF or both. SC–6 months or SM or both
Banks, recognized company of its holding company, failure to keep register of directors', loans, quasi-loans, etc	1980 57(6)	Director	I–UF SC–SM
Books, &c, dishonestly destroying or defacing, intent to cause loss	Theft Act 1968, s 18	Director, officer, manager, member	I–7 years or UF or both SC–6 months or SM or both
Books or registers, loose-leaf, failure to prevent falsification of	1948 436(2)	Company and every officer	SC–1/5 SM or Default fine
Business letters and order forms, failure to give required particulars including registered office, number and place	European Communities Act 1972 s 9(7)	Company and every officer or other person	SC–1/5 SM
Capital, serious loss, failure to convene meeting	1980 34(2)	Director	I–UF SC–SM
Certificate for shares, debentures, failure to deliver	1948 80(2)	Company and every officer	SC–1/5 SM or Default fine
Change of name; failure to comply with order to change	1948 18(2) 1967 46(4)	Company	SC–1/5 SM or Default fine
Change of name, not ceasing to use 'Chamber of Commerce' after revocation of licence	1948 19(7)	The body	I–UF SC–SM Default fine– 1/10 SM
Charges, failure to register particulars of creation of	1948 {96(3) 97(2)	Company and every officer	I–UF SC–SM or Default fine

Offence	Section	Person liable	Penalty
Charges, Register of, or instruments, refusal to allow inspection of	1948 {105(2) / 106 J(2)}	Every officer	SC–1/5 SM or Default fine
Charges, Register of, wilful failure to make entries in	1948 104(2)	Any officer	I–UF SC–SM
Charges, registration of, wilful and false statements in or failure to register changes. Scotland, omitting entry	1948 95 96 97 106 B(3) and C(2) 106 I(2)	Any person	I–UF SC–SM or Default fine 1/10
Class rights, failure to register particulars	1980 33(6)	Company and every officer	SC–1/5 SM or Default fine
Class rights, variation of; failure to register court's order	1948 72(5)	Company and every officer	SC–1/5 SM or Default fine
Commencement of business, restrictions contravened by public company	1980 4(7)	Director and every officer	I–UF SC–SM Directors liable to compensation order
Commission, failure to file statement as to	1948 53(5)	Company and every officer	SC–1/5 SM
Compensation for loss of office, failure to include details in offer of shares	1948 193(2)	Director or any person	SC–1/5 SM
Compromise or arrangement, failure to register office copy of order, or to annex copy to memorandum issued	1948 206(4)	Company and every officer	SC–1/5 SM
Compromise or arrangement, failure to reveal information	1948 207(4)	Company and every officer (including Liquidator and Trustee)	I–UF SC–SM

SUBJECT MATTER OF OFFENCE	ACT AND SECTION	PERSONS LIABLE	MAXIMUM PENALTY
Compromise or arrangement, failure by director or trustee or debenture holders to give notice of meeting	1948 207(5)	Company and every officer	SC–1/5 SM
Compromise or arrangement, failure to give notice of order to registrar	1948 208(3)	Company and every officer	SC–1/5 SM or Default fine
Contracts, failure to notify interest in	1948 199(4)	Director	I–UF SC–SM
Debenture, wilfully and knowingly issued without endorsement of certificate of registration	1948 99(2)	Any person	SC–1/5 SM
Declaration of solvency made without reasonable grounds for opinion stated therein	1948 283(3)	Director	I–6 months or UF or both SC–6 months or SM or both
Department of Trade, failure to comply with requirement to produce books or papers or an explanation or statement relating thereto	1967 109(4)	Company or any person	I–UF SC–SM
Department of Trade, fraudulent or reckless explanation or statement	1967 114(2)	Any person	I–2 years or UF or both SC–6 months or SM or both
Department of Trade, obstruction of entry and search under warrant issued to	1967 110(4)	Any person	I–UF SC–SM
Department of Trade, unauthorized publication of information obtained in course of exercise of powers of	1967 111(2)	Any person	I–2 years or UF or both SC–6 months or SM or both
Director; dealings in options by, in quoted shares or debentures of company of which a director, or of an associated company	1967 25(1)	Director	I–2 years or UF or both SC–6 months or SM or both

Offence	Act/Section	Persons liable	Penalty
Director or manager, failure to disclose unlimited liability of or notify proposed director or manager	1948 202(3)	Director, manager secretary	I–UF SC–SM
Director; failure to give notice of age, or acting as director after termination by reason of age	1948 186(2)	Director	SC–1/5 SM or Default fine
Directors, failure to enter particulars in trade catalogues, circulars	1948 201(3)	Every officer	SC–1/5 SM
Directors, failure to hold share qualifications	1948 182(5)	Director or former director	SC–1/5 SM or Default fine until last day proved he acted as a director
Directors' interests, failure by director to notify company of	1967 27(8)	Any person	I–2 years or UF or both SC–6 months or SM or both
Directors' interests, failure by company to notify recognized Stock Exchange of directors' dealings in listed securities	1976 25(3)	Company and every officer	SC–1/5 SM or Default fine
Director's loan or quasi-loan from company or guarantee or security provided for him, except as permitted	1980 53(5)	Any person	I–2 years or UF or both SC–6 months or SM or both
Directors' interests; failure to notify company of interests of spouse and infant children	1967 31(3)	Any person	I–2 years or UF or both SC–6 months or SM or both
Director. Disqualification. Acting in contravention of order not to be a director or concerned in management	Insolvency Act, 1976, s 9	Any person	I–2 years or UF or both SC–6 months or SM or both
Directors' interests, false statement by director in relation to	1967 27(8)	Any person	I–2 years or UF or both SC–6 months or SM or both

SUBJECT MATTER OF OFFENCE	ACT AND SECTION	PERSONS LIABLE	MAXIMUM PENALTY
Directors' report, failure to secure compliance with statutory requirements of	1967 23	Director	I–UF SC–SM
Directors' service contracts, failure to keep available for inspection at appropriate place	1967 26(5)	Company and every officer	SC–1/5 SM or Default fine
Directors' service contracts, failure to notify registrar of change of place where kept or inspection refused	1967 26(5)	Company and every officer	SC–1/5 SM or Default fine
Disclosure of salaries, pensions and loans, failure as directors	1948 198(4)	Any person	SC–1/5 SM
Disposal of books and papers of company, contravention of rules or directions of Department of Trade concerning	1948 341(4)	Any person	SC–1/5 SM
Dissolution of company, court's order declaring void; failure to register office copy of	1948 352(2)	Person making application	SC–1/5 SM or Default fine
Dissolution of company, failure to register court's order deferring voluntary winding up	1948 { 290(5) 300(5)	Person making application to court	SC–1/5 SM or Default fine
Documents relating to property or affairs of company, destruction, mutilation or falsification of, unless proved innocent or fraudulently parting with, altering or making an omission in	1967 113(1)(2)	Any officer	I–7 years or UF or both SC–6 months or SM or both
Dominion register, failure to keep duplicate	1948 120(7)	Company and every officer	SC–1/5 SM or Default fine

Offence	Act & section	Persons liable	Penalty
Dominion register, failure to notify situation	1948 119(3)	Company and every officer	SC–1/5 SM or Default fine
Expert report for allotment of shares by public company for non-cash, false statement by expert	1980 25(5)	Any person	I–2 years or UF or both SC–6 months or SM or both
Expert report for allotment of shares by public company for non-cash, failure to deliver report and resolution to Registrar	1980 27(2)	Company and every officer	SC–1/5 SM or Default fine
False statement in official return	Perjury Act 1911, s 5	Any person	I–2 years or UF or both SC–6 months or SM or both
Financial assistance by company for purchase of shares	1948 54(2)	Company and every officer	I–2 years or UF or both SC–6 months or SM or both
Fraudulent person failing to obey order to restrain from managing company	1948 188(6)	Any person	I–2 years or UF or both SC–6 months or SM or both
Fraudulent statement, making, &c	Theft Act 1968, s 19	Any officer	I–7 years or UF or both SC–6 months or SM or both
Holding or subsidiary company, failure to give information for purposes of audit to the other	1976 18	Company and every officer, auditor without reasonable excuse	SC–1/5 SM or Default fine
Increase in number of members of unlimited or guaranteed company, failure to register	1948 7(3)	Company and every officer	SC–1/5 SM or Default fine
Increase of capital, failure to register	1948 63(3)	Company and every officer	SC–1/5 SM or Default fine
Index of members, failure to keep	1948 111(4)	Company and every officer	SC–1/5 SM or Default fine
Insider-dealing, individual contravening ss 68 or 69 of 1980 Act	1980 72	Any individual	I–2 years or UF or both SC–6 months or SM or both Court has power to order compensation, restitution etc

SUBJECT MATTER OF OFFENCE	ACT AND SECTION	PERSONS LIABLE	MAXIMUM PENALTY
Inspection of books, where offence suspected	1948 441		Order to produce
Inspection of files of Registrar of companies; untrue representation of being a creditor or member	1948 426(4)	Any person	SC–1/5 SM
Inspector, failure to provide information about interests in shares or giving false information	1948 173(3)	Any person	SC–6 months or UF or both
Inspector, refusal to produce documents to, or answer questions of	1948 167(3)	Any officer or agent or body corporate	Punishment as contempt of court
Investment, distributing a prohibited circular relating to	Prevention of Fraud (Investments) Act 1958, s 14	Any person	1–2 years or UF or both SC–6 months or SM or both
Investment; fraudulently or recklessly inducing persons to invest money, or conspiring to commit such an offence	Prevention of Fraud (Investments) Act 1958, s 13	Any person	1–7 years or UF or both SC–6 years or SM or both
'Limited', use of, without incorporation	1948 439	Any person	SC–1/5 SM or Default fine
Limited, private company, using Welsh name form not also stating in English in business letters, papers, etc	1976 30(5)	Company and every officer	SC–1/5 SM
Members' resolutions or statements, failure to circulate	1948 140(7)	Every officer	SC–1/5 SM
Memorandum; alteration of objects by company, or application to court for alteration, failure to register	1948 5(8)	Company and every officer	SC–1/5 SM or Default fine

	European Communities Act 1972, s 9(5)	Company and every officer	SC–1/5 SM or Default fine
Memorandum or Articles, failure to send to Registrar print of amended copy of Memorandum or Articles or of any Act or statutory instrument altering the same			
Memorandum, failure to issue with alterations therein	1948 25(2)	Company and every officer	SC–1/5 SM
Memorandum or Articles, failure to send copy order altering or permitting alteration to Registrar on relief against unfair treatment of member	1980 75(7)	Company and every officer	SC–1/5 SM or Default fine
Memorandum and Articles, or any Act of Parliament altering, failure to supply on demand	1948 24(2)	Company and every officer	SC–1/5 SM
Minute books, failure to keep	1948 145(4)	Company and every officer	SC–1/5 SM or Default fine
Minute books of general meetings, failure to allow inspection or supply copies of entries in	1948 146(3)	Company	SC–1/5 SM Court may compel immediate compliance
Name of company, carrying on business as a public limited company or as private company when not so entitled	1980 76(4)	Any person	SC–1/5 SM or Default fine
Name of company, failure to place on business letters etc, or in legible characters on seal	1948 108(3)(4)	Company and every officer	SC–1/5 SM
Name of company, failure by Welsh public company to place on business letters, etc in English that it is a public limited company	1980 (7)	Company and every officer	SC–1/5 SM or Default fine
Old public company, failure to obtain new classification	1980 9(2)	Company and every officer	SC–1/5 SM or Default fine

SUBJECT MATTER OF OFFENCE	ACT AND SECTION	PERSONS LIABLE	MAXIMUM PENALTY
Name of company, failure to publish name outside office	1948 108(2)	Company and every officer	SC–1/5 SM or Default fine
Oversea company, business under corporate name in contravention of direction	1976 31(5)	Company and every officer or agent	I–UF SC–SM or Default fine
Oversea company, failure to register documents etc, or wilfully making false statements in documents	1948 407 to 414	Company, every officer or agent	SC–1/5 SM or Default fine
Personation of shareholder or creditor, untruthfully, to see statement of affairs or comments of receiver or manager	1948 426(4)	Any person	SC–1/5 SM
Prospectus, issue of, by oversea company; various defaults	1948 417 to 421	Any person	I–UF SC–SM
Prospectus, issue of unregistered	1948 41(4)	Company and every person	SC–1/5 SM or Default fine
Prospectus, issuing form of application without	1948 38(3)	Any person	SC–SM I–UF
Prospectus, knowingly issuing containing expert's report without consent	1948 40(2)	Company and every person a party	SC–SM I–UF
Prospectus, untrue statements in (unless immaterial)	1948 44(1)	Any person	I–2 years or UF or both SC–6 months or SM or both
Proxies, failure to state in notice of meeting that members may appoint	1948 136(2)	Every officer	SC–1/5 SM
Proxies, sending invitations to some members only	1948 136(4)	Every officer	SC–1/5 SM

Public company or old public company, failure to comply with procedures for re-registration as private	1980 11(10)	Company and every officer	SC–1/5 SM or Default fine
Public company, failure to reduce or cancel share capital or re-register as private when obliged to do so	1980 37(7)	Company and every officer	SC–1/5 SM or Default fine
Purchase by company of own shares contrary to permitted exceptions	1980 35(3)	Company and every officer	Company I–UF SC–SM Officer I–2 years or UF or both SC–6 months or SM or both
Receiver or manager, failure to give notice of appointment or cesser	1948 102(3)	Any person	SC–1/5 SM or Default fine
Receiver or manager, corporate body acting as	1948 366	Body	I–UF SC–SM
Receiver or manager, failure to name on invoices	1948 370(2)	Any officers, liquidator, or receiver	SC–1/5 SM
Receiver or manager, failure to register accounts	1948 374(2)	Receiver	SC–1/5 SM or Default fine
Register of directors' interests, failure to inscribe relevant information within three days in	1967 29(12)		
Register of directors' interests, failure to keep in proper form	1967 29(12)	Company and every officer	SC–1/5 SM or Default fine
Register of directors' interests, failure to notify Registrar of change of place where kept	1967 29(12)		
Register of members, failure to allow inspection or send extracts of	1948 113(3)	Company and every officer	SC–1/5 SM

SUBJECT MATTER OF OFFENCE	ACT AND SECTION	PERSONS LIABLE	MAXIMUM PENALTY
Register of members, failure to keep or notify place where kept	1948 110(4)	Company and every officer	SC–1/5 SM or Default fine
Register of substantial individual interests, failure to allow inspection, send copies, inscribe relevant information within three days or failure to keep in proper form	1967 34(8)	Company and every officer	SC–1/5 SM or Default fine. Court may order immediate compliance
Receiver or manager, failure to register appointment and send notices and statements	1948 372(7)	Receiver	SC–1/5 SM or Default fine
Receivers' statement of affairs, failure to supply information	1948 373(5)	Any person	SC–1/5 SM or Default fine
Reduction of capital, wilful concealment of name of creditor or misrepresentation of debt	1948 71	Any officer	I–UF SC–SM
Register of debenture-holders, refusal of inspection of	1948 87(4)	Company and every officer	SC–1/5 SM or Default fine. Court may order immediate inspection
Register of directors and secretaries, failure to keep or allow inspection of	1948 200(7)	Company and every officer	SC–1/5 SM or Default fine
Register of directors' interests, failure to allow to keep, allow inspection, notify location, index, provide copies or display at annual general meeting	1967 29(12)	Company and every officer	SC–1/5 SM or (except for failure to produce register and keep it accessible at meeting) Default fine. Court may order immediate compliance
Registered office, failure to have or file notice of change	1976 23(4)	Company and every officer	SC–1/5 SM or Default fine
Resolutions, failure to annex to articles and supply on demand	1948 143(6)	Company and every officer	SC–1/5 SM or Default fine

Offence	Section	Liable	Penalty
Resolutions, failure to register a copy in the form approved by the Registrar	1948 143(5) 1967 51(2)	Company and every officer	SC–1/5 SM or Default fine
Restrictions on shares imposed by Department of Trade, disposal, voting or failure to give required notice	1948 174(5)	Any person	SC–6 months or UF or both
Restrictions on shares imposed by Department of Trade, issue in contravention	1948 174(6)	Company and every officer	I–UF SC–SM
Seal of company, failure to engrave	1948 108(2)	Company	SC–1/5 SM
Share capital, failure to give notice of consolidation, conversion, division, redemption, cancellation of	1948 62(2)	Company and every officer	SC–1/5 SM or Default fine
Share warrants, forgery in Scotland of	1948 85(1)	Any person	I–7 years or UF or both SC–6 months or SM or both
Share warrants, engraved without lawful authority, in Scotland	1948 85(2)	Any person	I–7 years or UF or both SC–6 months or SM or both
Substantial individual interests, failure to disclose or false statement with relation to	1967 33(6)	Any person	I–2 years or UF or both SC–6 months or SM or both
Transfer of shares, failure to send notice of refusal	1948 78(2)	Company and every officer	SC–1/5 SM or Default fine

Part II—Offences on Winding-up

SUBJECT MATTER OF OFFENCE	ACT AND SECTION	PERSONS LIABLE	MAXIMUM PENALTY
Agreement with creditors, obtaining by false representations	1948 328(1)(*p*)	Past or present officer	I–7 years or UF or both SC–6 months or SM or both
Altering or omitting entries in books or papers	1948 328(1)(*k*)		
Body corporate acting as liquidator or as receiver	1948 335(*b*) 366	Body corporate	I–UF SC–SM
Books and papers, concealing, destroying, mutilating or falsifying	1948 328(1)(*i*)	Past or present officer	I–7 years or UF or both SC–6 months or SM or both
Books and papers, failure to deliver to liquidator	1948 328(1)(*c*)		
Books and papers, preventing production of	1948 328(1)(*h*)		
Carrying on of business fraudulently	1948 332(3)	Any person	I–7 years or UF or both SC–6 months or SM or both
Credit, obtaining by falsely representing that company is carrying on business	1948 328(1)(*n*)	Past or present officer	I–7 years or UF or both SC–6 months or SM or both
Credit, obtaining by fraud	1948 328(1)(*m*)		
Creditors' voluntary winding-up, failure to call first meeting of creditors, advertise or produce statement	1948 293(6)	Company or directors	I–UF SC–SM

Offence	Section	Person	Penalty
Debts, concealment of	1948 328(1)(d)	Past or present officer	Two years
Declaration of solvency, failure of liquidator to call meeting of creditors if company unable to pay debts in named time	1948 288(2)	Liquidator	SC–1/5 SM
Destroying books, &c	1948 341(4)	Any person	SC–1/5 SM
Director, false statement of solvency without reasonable grounds	1948 283(3)	Director	I–6 months or UF or both SC–6 months or SM or both
Directors, acting contrary to rules given for presentation by Department of Trade	1948 274(3)	Liquidator	SC–1/5 SM or Default fine
Dissolution, failure of liquidator to register order or order declaration dissolution void	1948 352(2)	Liquidator	SC–1/5 SM or Default fine
Document, altering, parting with, omitting from	1948 328(1)(k)	Past or present officer	I–7 years or UF or both SC–6 months or SM or both
Entry, fraudulent, in books, &c	1948 329	Officer or contributory	I–7 years or UF or both SC–6 months or SM or both
False debt, failure to reveal proof of	1948 328(1)(g)	Past or present officer	I–7 years or UF or both SC–6 months or SM or both
False entry, making in any books or paper	1948 328(1)(j)	Past or present officer	I–7 years or UF or both SC–6 months or SM or both
Fraud, by officer of company in liquidation	1948 330	Officer	I–2 years or UF or both SC–6 months or SM or both
Inducing credit	1948 330	Officer	I–2 years or UF or both SC–6 months or SM or both

SUBJECT MATTER OF OFFENCE	ACT AND SECTION	PERSONS LIABLE	MAXIMUM PENALTY
Invoices, orders, business letters—failure to state that company in liquidation	1948 338(2)	Officer, liquidator, receiver or manager	SC–1/5 SM
Liquidator, appointment, failure to gazette and register notice of	1948 305(2)	Liquidator	SC–1/5 SM or Default fine
Liquidator, failure to summon meeting of creditors in case of insolvency or general meeting of members each year	1948 288(2) 289(2) 299(2)	Liquidator	SC–1/5 SM
Liquidator, failure to send Registrar account and return of final meeting or copy order deferring date of dissolution of statement of position if not concluded within 1 year of commencement	1948 290(3) 290(5) 303(3) 305(5) 342(2)	Liquidator	SC–1/5 SM or Default fine
Liquidator, offer to secure or prevent nomination or appointment corruptly	1948 336	Any person	I–UF SC–SM
Liquidator, final meeting, failure to call	1948 290(6) 300(6)	Liquidator	SC–1/5 SM
Liquidator, accounts failure to register	1948 342(2)	Liquidator	SC–1/5 SM Default fine

Offence	Section	Person liable	Penalty
Losses or expenses, fictitious	1948 328(1)(l)	Past or present officer	1–7 years or UF or both SC–6 months or SM or both
Omission, material, from statement of affairs	1948 328(1)(f)		
Property of company, failure to deliver to liquidator	1948 328(1)(b)		
Property of company, failure to reveal to liquidator	1948 328(1)(a)		
Property of company, fraudulent removal of	1948 328(1)		
Property of company, £10 and over, concealing	1948 328(1)		
Receiving pawned or pledged property of company	1948 328(2)	Any person	Seven years
Registers, books, documents or securities, destroying, mutilating, altering, falsifying	1948 329	Any officer or contributory	1–7 years or UF or both SC–6 months or SM or both
Resolution to wind up, failure to gazette	1948 279(2)	Company, officer and liquidator	SC–1/5 SM or Default fine
Statement of affairs, failure to make out	1948 235(5)	Any person	I–UF SC–SM or Default fine 1/10 SM
Statement of affairs, inspection, false statement applicant a creditor or contributory	1948 235(7)	Any person	As for contempt of court

Table 11

Rights and obligations by size of shareholding

Note: This list is not exhaustive and where problems arise professional advice should be taken as to the particular circumstances.

SIZE OF SHAREHOLDING	RIGHTS AND OBLIGATIONS
Any shareholding	To sue for fraud or infringement of individual rights or complain of fraudulent or oppressive conduct to the Department of Trade where breach of specific statutory duties are involved:
5%+	(i) To insist that meetings be held only after due notice; (ii) In case of quoted public companies, obligation to give notice to the company of sale or purchase of shares.
10%+	To requisition extraordinary general meetings and to demand polls.
15%+	(i) To apply to Court to cancel variation of class rights within specific time; (ii) In case of quoted public companies if bought within previous twelve months and making takeover bid obligations to offer the highest price paid for any of the shares bought.
20%+	To consolidate profits and the duty to do so in case of quoted public companies if the holding company participates in management.
25%+	To block special resolutions on any account.
30%+	In case of quoted public companies if purchasing in concert with others a total holding of 30% of voting shares, obligation to bid for the rest. If the holding is more than 30% and the holding is increased by more than 2% in any year the like obligation unless and until the holding is more than 50%.
35%+	If held by the general public the company may escape treatment as a close company.
50%+	(i) To pass ordinary resolutions including the right to appoint or dismiss directors or auditors and to elect chairmen; (ii) An obligation to produce group accounts; (iii) To have a group registration for VAT; (iv) Advance corporation tax need not be paid on dividends to holding companies; (v) To elect for group treatment for dividends.

75%+	(i) To pass all resolutions without right of minority to object, except in case of a variation of class rights or of fraud or oppression;
	(ii) To amend the Memorandum and Articles of Association except in case of class rights fraud or oppression;
	(iii) To remove directors without special notice;
	(iv) If a holding company, to make or take transfers of assets up or down without capital gains tax liability and to transfer the benefit of tax relief or losses capital allowances and the like or to transfer from one 75% subsidiary to another.
85%+	To vary on share rights in absence of fraud or oppression.
90%+	(i) To refuse to call extraordinary general meetings;
	(ii) To accept a bid upon terms which in the absence of fraud must be accepted by remaining minority.
95%+	To hold meetings at short notice or waiving formal notice.

Index